SAXONY
NARROW GAUGE
featuring the extensive 75cm,
60cm and 38cm lines

John Organ
Series editor Vic Mitchell

MP Middleton Press

Front Cover: Still carrying its old DR number 99 738, a Class VIIK alt 2-10-2T is about to depart from Dippoldiswalde on 5th August 1963. At that time the station still retained the platform roof canopies protecting the waiting passengers from the elements. (D.Trevor Rowe)

Rear Cover: 75cm gauge Saxon-Meyer no. 99 535 was refuelled at Hetzdorf from a makeshift loading stage in August 1967. The pulleys for the Heberlein brake cable can be seen on the rear of the cab, the early braking system being still in use on the line until it closed four months after this photograph was recorded. (T.Martin).

An atmospheric scene was recorded at Mügeln as Saxon-Meyer no. 099 708 (DR no. 99 582) had its fire removed outside the depot, whilst sister locomotive no. 099 713 (99 608) passed with a freight from Oschatz during an April evening in 1992. (B.Benn)

Published January 2005

ISBN 1 904474 47 0

© *Middleton Press, 2005*

Design Deborah Esher

Printed & bound by Biddles Ltd, Kings Lynn

Published by
  Middleton Press
  Easebourne Lane
  Midhurst, West Sussex
  GU29 9AZ
Tel: 01730 813169
Fax: 01730 812601
Email: info@middletonpress.co.uk
www.middletonpress.co.uk

CONTENTS

PART ONE.   THE 75cm NETWORK IN SAXONY

1. SAXON STATE RAILWAYS
2. SAXON NARROW GAUGE LOCOMOTIVE DEVELOPMENT
3. FREITAL HAINSBERG – KURORT KIPSDORF
4. RADEBEUL – RADEBURG
5. OSCHATZ – MÜGELN – KEMMLITZ
6. ZITTAU – KURORT OYBIN AND KURORT JONSDORF
7. CRANZAHL – KURORT OBERWIESENTHAL
8. PRESERVATION IN SAXONY:
     OBERRITTERSGRÜN
     SCHÖNHEIDE
     PRESSNITZTALBAHN

PART TWO.   FORESTRY AND PARK RAILWAYS

9. WALDEISENBAHN MUSKAU
10. SÄCHSEN PARKEISENBAHN

ACKNOWLEDGEMENTS

During the course of compiling this publication, along with its companion volume North East German Narrow Gauge, I have once again been very fortunate in having received much valuable assistance from many people. My thanks are therefore due to Mr and Mrs B.Benn, Mr.J.Dobson, Mr.A.Heywood, Mr.J.Marsh, Mr.T.Martin, Mr.D.Trevor Rowe, Mr.B.Rumary, Mr K.Taylorson and Mr. J.Wiseman. Finally I must once again add a special word of thanks to my wife Brenda who has, as usual, tolerated my deep involvement in the subject during the period of research and compilation.

1. FREITAL HAINSBERG – KURORT KIPSDORF.
2. RADEBEUL ÖST – RADEBURG.
3. OSCHATZ – MÜGELN – KEMMLITZ.
4. ZITTAU – KURORT OYBIN / JONSDORF.
5. CRANZAHL – KURORT OBERWIESENTHAL.
6. SCHÖNHEIDE MUSEUMBAHN.
7. PRESSNITZTALBAHN.
8. WALDEISENBAHN MUSKAU.
9. DRESDEN PARKEISENBAHN.
10. LEIPZIG PARKEISENBAHN AUENSEE.
11. COTTBUS PARKEISENBAHN.

INTRODUCTION

Germany boasted a colossal network of narrow gauge railways during the 19th Century and first half of the 20th Century. Although found throughout the country, the largest proliferation was in the north and east, in what became East Germany following the upheaval of World War 2. Following the creation of the German Democratic Republic (GDR), the large systems in Saxony, Harz and Baltic regions were all controlled by the state system Deutsche Reichsbahn (DR) until the reunification of Germany in 1990. Between 1920 and 1945, the Saxon lines had been under the control of the predecessor of DR, Deutsche Reichsbahn-Gesellschaft (DRG).

The majority of lines that remained in West Germany were closed during the 1950s and 1960s, as part of modernisation and co-ordination schemes. However, many of those in East Germany were saved as a result of the severe austerity implemented by the communist government and lack of investment to modernise the rail network. Consequently when the two countries were reunited and the former DR systems were transferred either to Deutsche Bahn (DB) or newly formed private consortiums, there existed a veritable "time warp" of narrow gauge railways still relying on steam haulage and providing an everyday service of both passenger and freight trains. Needless to say the decade since reunification has by necessity seen many changes, although steam still reigns supreme on the surviving lines. The locomotives are mainly powerful 2-10-2Ts, many of which were built during the 1950s, together with articulated machines in the form of historic 0-4-4-0T Meyers of an earlier vintage.

As mentioned above, the majority of the lines that survived into the 1990s were to be absorbed by the private sector and rely mainly on the tourist industry for most of their custom. Those that have remained under state control are probably living on "borrowed time" as DB are under pressure to close or dispose of its remaining narrow gauge lines. Sadly, one of the Saxon DB controlled lines, and also one of the most scenic, was badly damaged by the floods that struck Eastern Europe in 2002 and was partly closed prematurely. However, support from the locality for the rebuilding of the damaged section is very vociferous and hopefully the line will be rebuilt and reopened by a private consortium in the not too distant future. Recent information has confirmed that the line is to be completely rebuilt as soon as possible, although future ownership is yet to be decided.

In a publication of this size it would be impossible to cover all the narrow gauge railways in a large country the size of Germany. Consequently it will concentrate upon a selection of the systems that were formerly behind the Iron Curtain in the GDR, of which many have survived to become a mecca for steam enthusiasts world-wide. The systems covered in this volume include the extensive 75cm gauge railways throughout Saxony, together with an important 60cm forestry system and the pioneering miniature lines situated in the parks of the major cities. The large metre gauge network in the Harz Mountains and the many lines of various gauges in the Baltic and Brandenburg regions are covered in the companion volume, North East German Narrow Gauge.

Despite the austere conditions that the citizens of the GDR were forced to endure, it is gratifying to record that the East German Government appreciated the historic nature of the surviving narrow gauge railways within their country. In 1975, all the remaining lines in the area covered by this publication were accorded the status of National Technical Monuments, a fact that has undoubtedly assisted their continued survival into the 21st Century. Even so, some of these lines were threatened with closure around the time of reunification, one line having closed in 1986 due to a lack of finance to implement much needed repair work. Fortunately closure of the surviving lines proved unnecessary due to the political upheaval, which allowed time for a complete review of the situation.

PART ONE - THE 75cm NETWORK IN SAXONY
1. Saxon State Railways.

Between 1881 and 1923, a comprehensive network of 75cm railways was opened throughout Saxony, or Sächsen as it is known in German. Constructed by the Saxon State Railways, these eventually totalled 556km by 1923 when the last short branches were opened by DRG, who had absorbed the Saxon lines in 1920. Whilst two of the lines were converted to standard gauge, one as early as 1897, the other in 1938, the remainder provided an invaluable service as feeders to the main line system. They were situated in the eastern part of Germany, close to the Polish and Czech borders of more recent times, with Dresden and Chemnitz at the centre of the systems.

Most of the lines were fairly short isolated branches, providing interchange facilities with the standard gauge at the principal termini. However many of these lines were eventually connected around the turn of the century, which created a comprehensive network of narrow gauge routes. The majority of this network was situated to the west of Dresden, a major 75cm gauge junction being created at the small town of Wilsdruff which lay in the centre of the system.

The lines in the northern part of the network, such as those radiating from Wilsdruff and the outskirts of Dresden, were principally freight carrying lines. Their passenger services were in the main for the benefit of commuters, with early morning and late evening "workers trains" as a routine necessity. In the south of the area where the lines terminated at spa towns, high in the Erzgebirge (Ore Mountains) close to the present day border with the Czech Republic, passenger traffic was the principal source of revenue. Freight traffic, in the form of domestic commodities, such as coal, were still an everyday occurrence although not to such a large degree as on the lines to the north.

Apart from the two lines converted to standard gauge, the 75cm system survived the rigours of two World Wars to find itself situated within the newly constituted GDR in 1949. The control of the railways had already been transferred from the Deutsche Reichsbahn-Gesellschaft (DRG) to the newly formed Deutsche Reichsbahn (DR) in 1945. With the severe restrictions imposed by the GDR upon its people and financial hardships endured by its industry, it was not surprising that many of these minor railway routes were forced to close due to lack of investment during this period of austerity. By the time of reunification in 1990, only five lines of this once extensive network had survived, with a total route distance of 86km. With the amalgamation of DR and DB into the reformed Deutsche Bahn, it was soon recognised that these survivors from an earlier age would have no place in a modernised integrated rail system.

The initial closures took place in 1945, with a few more during the 1950s. However the major escalation took place between 1964 and 1986, with lines closing on a regular basis. This was often as a result of the necessity for repairs to the permanent way or equipment, for which no money was available from DR. The state owned railway system periodically published a "Five Year Plan", which took a close look at its minor lines and recommended closure rather than expenditure for any which were in need of more than routine maintenance.

The first, and ultimately longest, of the isolated branches was opened in stages from Wilkau-Hasslau to Carlsfeld, in the foothills of the Erzgebirge, between 1881 and 1897. The 41.85km line was closed in sections between 1967 and 1979 although a 5km stretch of the southern section near Schönheide has survived to become a short "museum" line. In the same vicinity, the very scenic 22.95km route from Wolkenstein to Jöhstadt was a late casualty of the DR closure schemes. Opened in 1892, it survived until 1986, when it closed due to a fall in receipts and lack of maintenance. Fortunately 8km of the route was to be saved by another preservation group based at Jöhstadt, near the Czech border.

The mainly freight carrying lines to the west of Dresden, which were gradually connected between 1886 and 1913, largely ceased to exist by 1972. That year saw the demise of the important junction and depot at Wilsdruff, which has been described as the narrow gauge equivalent of Crewe. From this very complex network of lines, only two lines survived into the 1990s. The 18km section linking Kemmlitz, Mügeln and Oschatz together with the 26.66km between Freital-Hainsberg and Kurort Kipsdorf were the only remnants of this once extensive system to remain in operation after the reunification of Germany in 1990. In addition three isolated lines have also survived into the 21st Century. The 16.55km line north of Dresden linking Radebeul and Radeburg continued to provide a useful commuter service whilst the 14.40km route near the Polish border at Zittau, with two branches to Kurort Jonsdorf and Kurort Oybin, served an area somewhat devoid of other forms of public transport. Finally the scenic 17.35km line between Cranzahl and Kurort Oberwiesenthal continued to provide an invaluable service for those wishing to enjoy the mountain pursuits provided by the area in the vicinity of the southern terminus.

Saxon 75cm lines up to 1923
(B.Benn)

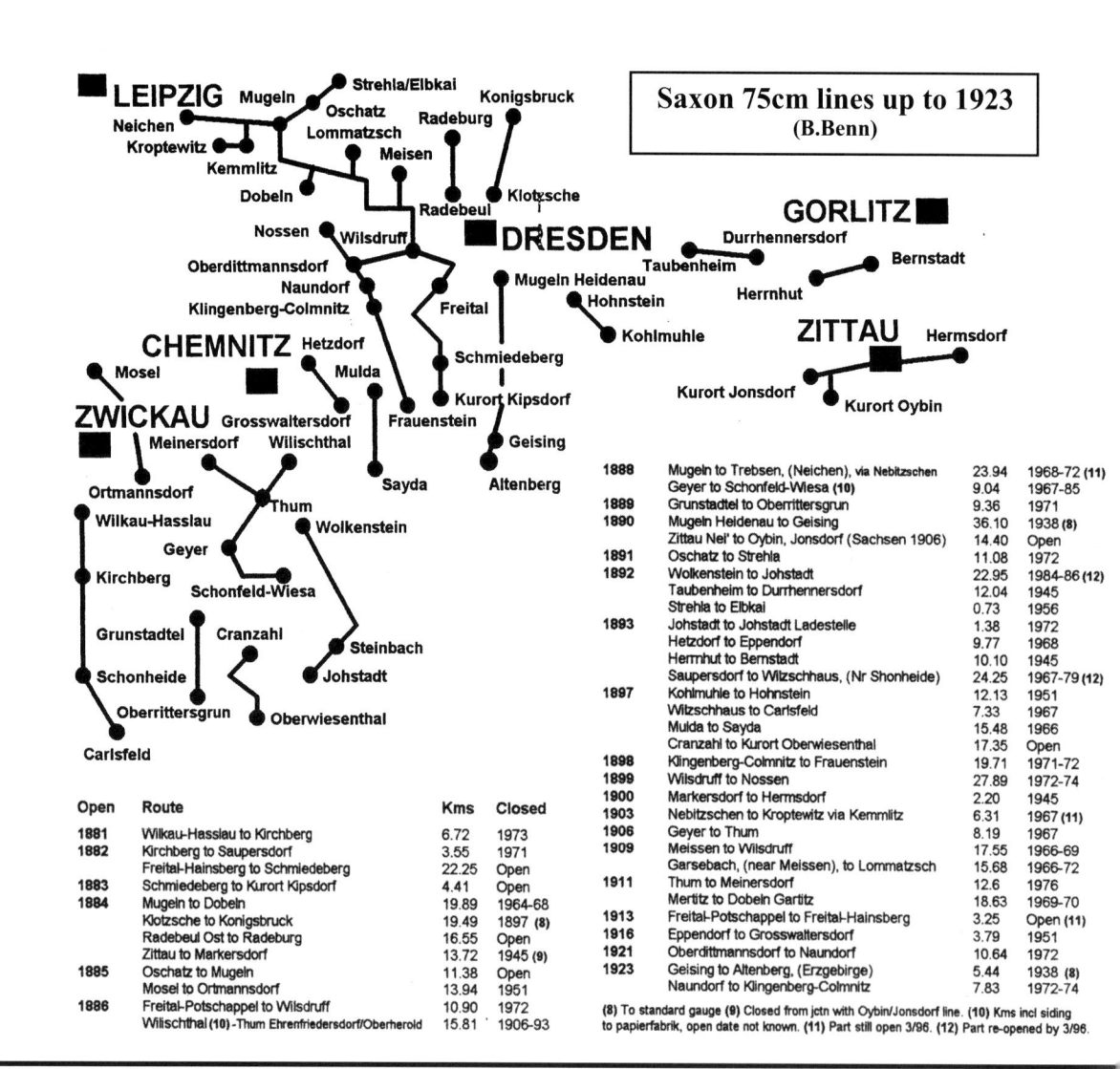

Map locations:
- LEIPZIG, Mugeln, Strehla/Elbkai, Konigsbruck
- Neichen, Oschatz, Radeburg
- Kroptewitz, Lommatzsch
- Kemmlitz, Meisen
- Dobeln, Klotzsche
- Nossen, Radebeul
- Wilsdruff, DRESDEN, GORLITZ
- Oberdittmannsdorf, Durrhennersdorf, Bernstadt
- Naundorf, Taubenheim
- Klingenberg-Colmnitz, Mugeln Heidenau, Herrnhut
- Freital, Hohnstein
- CHEMNITZ, Hetzdorf, Kohlmuhle, ZITTAU, Hermsdorf
- Mosel, Mulda, Schmiedeberg
- ZWICKAU, Grosswaltersdorf, Kurort Kipsdorf, Kurort Jonsdorf, Kurort Oybin
- Meinersdorf, Wilischthal, Frauenstein
- Ortmannsdorf, Sayda, Geising
- Wilkau-Hasslau, Thum, Altenberg
- Geyer, Wolkenstein
- Kirchberg, Schonfeld-Wiesa
- Grunstadtel, Cranzahl, Steinbach
- Schonheide, Johstadt
- Oberrittersgrun, Oberwiesenthal
- Carlsfeld

Open	Route	Kms	Closed
1881	Wilkau-Hasslau to Kirchberg	6.72	1973
1882	Kirchberg to Saupersdorf	3.55	1971
	Freital-Hainsberg to Schmiedeberg	22.25	Open
1883	Schmiedeberg to Kurort Kipsdorf	4.41	Open
1884	Mugeln to Dobeln	19.89	1964-68
	Klotzsche to Konigsbruck	19.49	1897 (8)
	Radebeul Ost to Radeburg	16.55	Open
	Zittau to Markersdorf	13.72	1945 (9)
1885	Oschatz to Mugeln	11.38	Open
	Mosel to Ortmannsdorf	13.94	1951
1886	Freital-Potschappel to Wilsdruff	10.90	1972
	Wilischthal (10) - Thum Ehrenfriedersdorf/Oberherold	15.81	1906-93
1888	Mugeln to Trebsen, (Neichen), via Nebitzschen	23.94	1968-72 (11)
	Geyer to Schonfeld-Wiesa (10)	9.04	1967-85
1889	Grunstadtel to Oberrittersgrun	9.36	1971
1890	Mugeln Heidenau to Geising	36.10	1938 (8)
	Zittau Nei' to Oybin, Jonsdorf (Sachsen 1906)	14.40	Open
1891	Oschatz to Strehla	11.08	1972
1892	Wolkenstein to Johstadt	22.95	1984-86 (12)
	Taubenheim to Durrhennersdorf	12.04	1945
	Strehla to Elbkai	0.73	1956
1893	Johstadt to Johstadt Ladestelle	1.38	1972
	Hetzdorf to Eppendorf	9.77	1968
	Herrnhut to Bernstadt	10.10	1945
	Saupersdorf to Wilzschhaus, (Nr Shonheide)	24.25	1967-79 (12)
1897	Kohlmuhle to Hohnstein	12.13	1951
	Witzschhaus to Carlsfeld	7.33	1967
	Mulda to Sayda	15.48	1966
	Cranzahl to Kurort Oberwiesenthal	17.35	Open
1898	Klingenberg-Colmnitz to Frauenstein	19.71	1971-72
1899	Wilsdruff to Nossen	27.89	1972-74
1900	Markersdorf to Hermsdorf	2.20	1945
1903	Nebitzschen to Kroptewitz via Kemmlitz	6.31	1967 (11)
1906	Geyer to Thum	8.19	1967
1909	Meissen to Wilsdruff	17.55	1966-69
	Garsebach, (near Meissen), to Lommatzsch	15.68	1966-72
1911	Thum to Meinersdorf	12.6	1976
	Mertitz to Dobeln Gartitz	18.63	1969-70
1913	Freital-Potschappel to Freital-Hainsberg	3.25	Open (11)
1916	Eppendorf to Grosswaltersdorf	3.79	1951
1921	Oberdittmannsdorf to Naundorf	10.64	1972
1923	Geising to Altenberg, (Erzgebirge)	5.44	1938 (8)
	Naundorf to Klingenberg-Colmnitz	7.83	1972-74

(8) To standard gauge (9) Closed from jctn with Oybin/Jonsdorf line. (10) Kms incl siding to papierfabrik, open date not known. (11) Part still open 3/96. (12) Part re-opened by 3/96.

(lower left) 1.1. A class 1VK 0-4-4-0T Saxon-Meyer no. 99 603 crosses the viaduct at Mulda on the line to Sayda, which closed in 1966. Note that most of the passengers on the leading coach were occupying the rear balcony in this scene from 6th August 1963. (D.Trevor Rowe).

1.2. No. 99 603 was recorded later the same day during the same journey, whilst replenishing its water tanks at Volgtsdorf. A small wagon, that appears to be very much like a track maintenance tool van, had been added to the train during the course of the journey. (D.Trevor Rowe).

1.3. LKM class V11K neu 2-10-2T no. 99 779 is about to depart from Meinersdorf with a train to Thum during a very wet evening on 8th August 1963. This branch of the system based around Thum closed in 1976 after an operating life of 65 years. (D.Trevor Rowe).

1.4. The main line of the Thum system that ran south to Geyer and Schonfeld-Wiesa closed in 1967, apart from a siding at the extreme southern end retained for use by a paper works. As a reminder of happier days, Meyer no. 99 534 and two coaches have been displayed in the restored station at Geyer since 1976, as recorded on 18th May 2004. (J.F.Organ).

1.5. Another Saxon-Meyer no. 99 551 was preparing to depart from Hetzdorf with a mixed train bound for Eppendorf on 9th August 1963. Note the Heberlein brake cable fitted to the locomotive and still in use on that line. (D.Trevor Rowe).

1.6. Before departing, the driver carried out a final oiling of the motion; note the oil cabinet incorporated into the side tank. Whilst this is taking place the Meyer was dwarfed by standard gauge locomotive no. 58 1765 as it passed on the adjacent line. (D.Trevor Rowe).

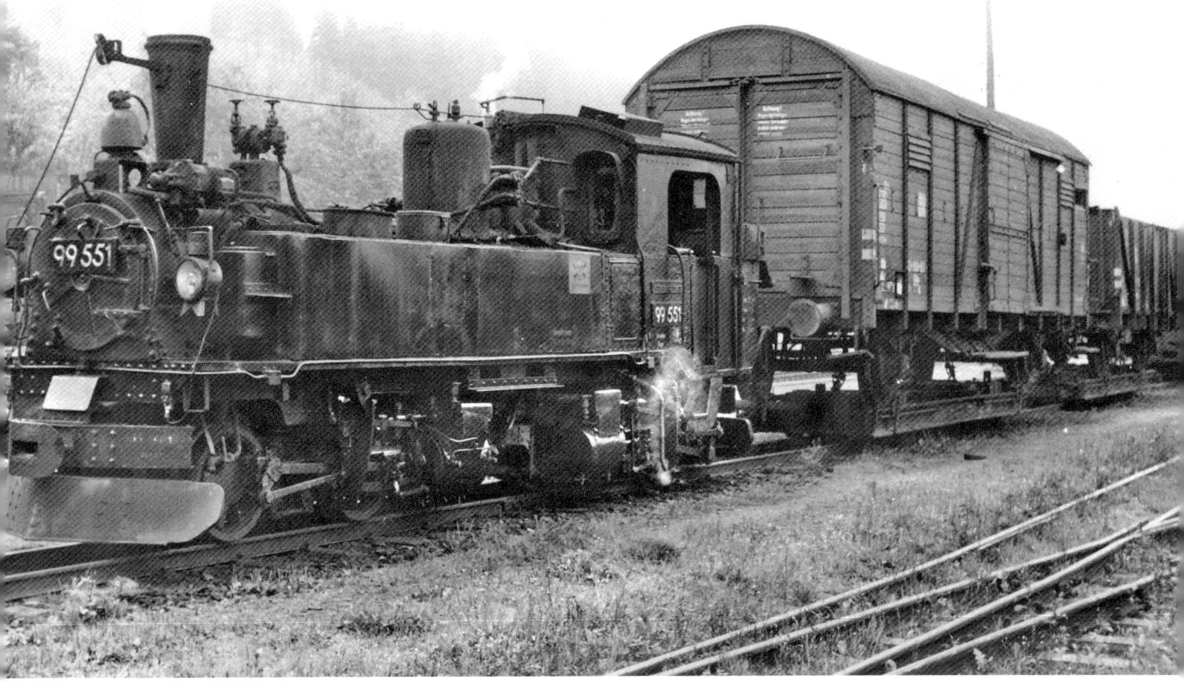
99 551
99 551

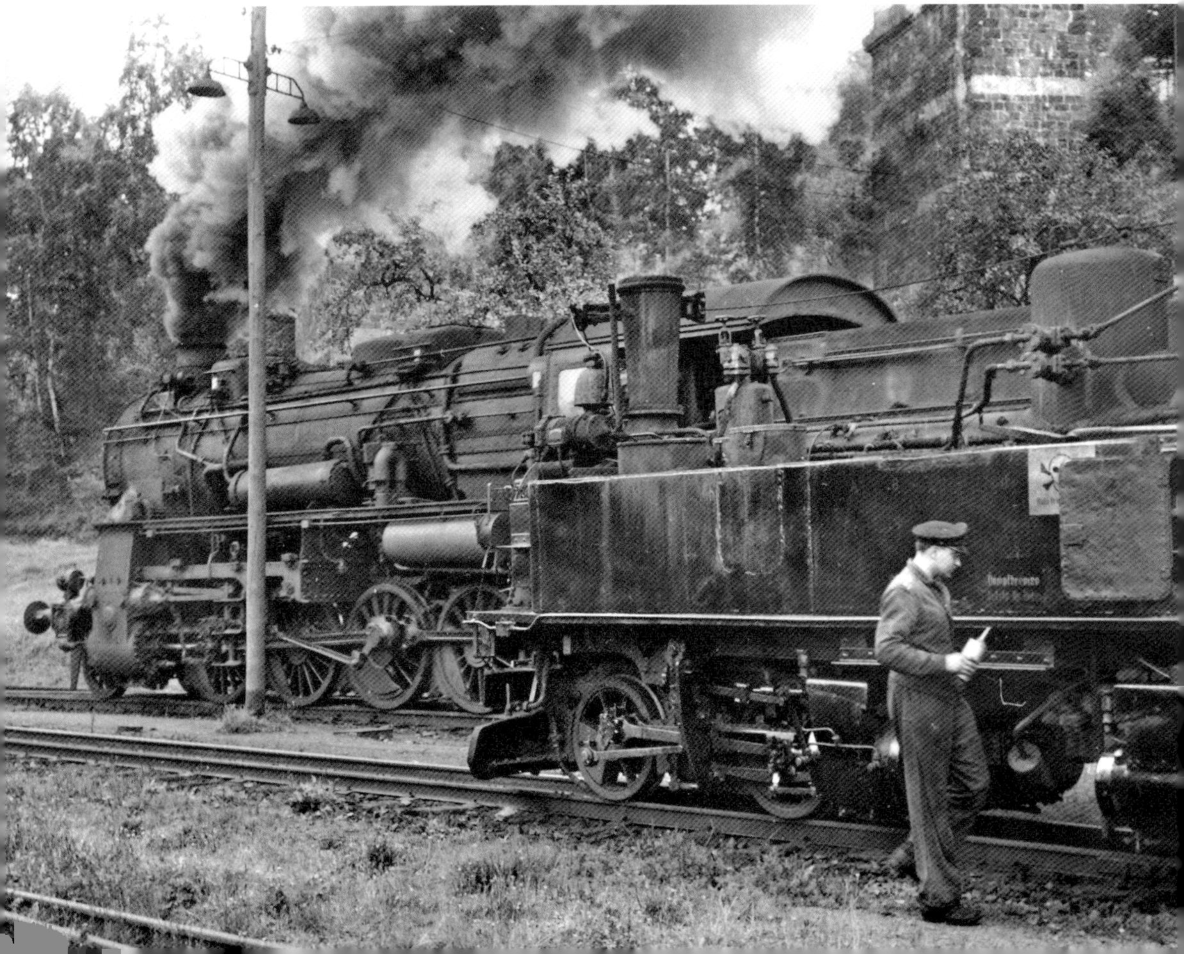

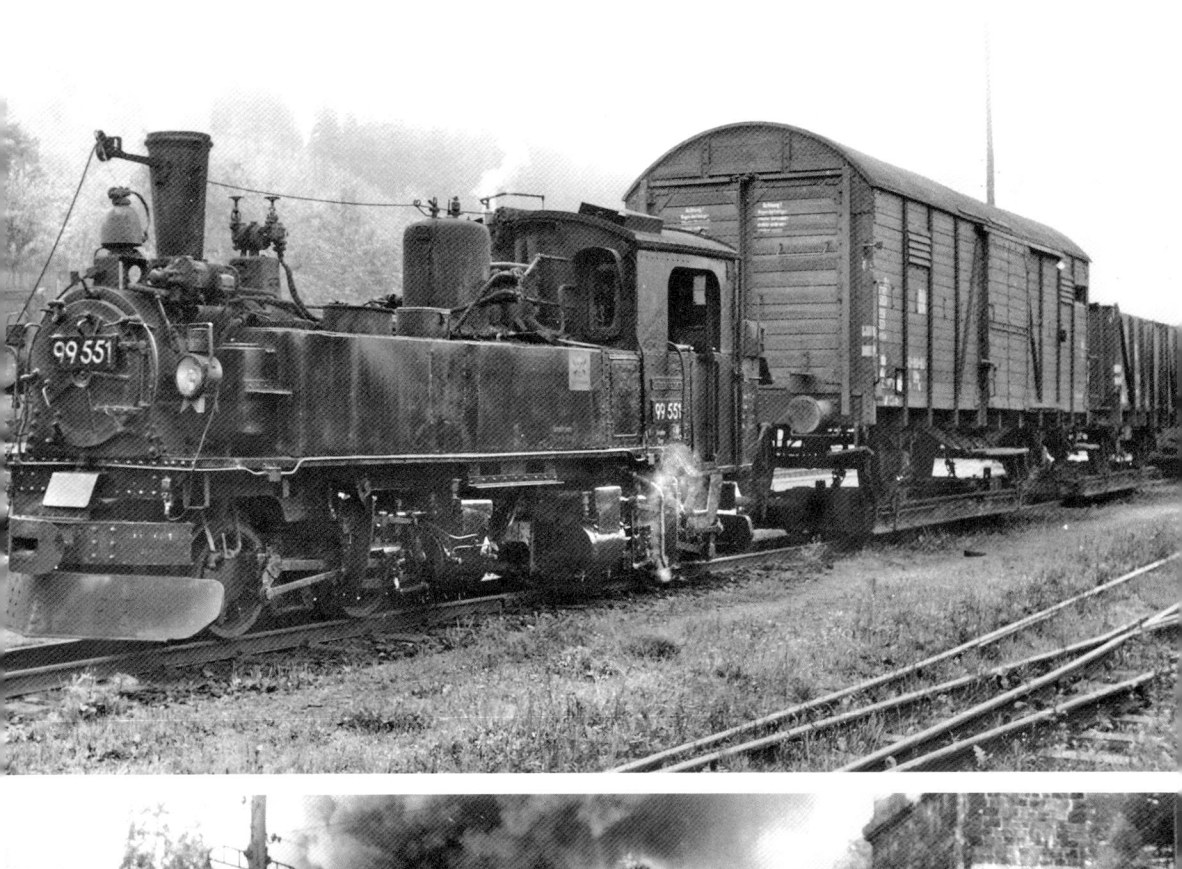

1.7. No. 99 551 made an impressive departure from Hetzdorf on the same occasion. The viaduct carries the main line linking Dresden and Chemnitz from which a standard gauge branch used to wind down into the valley to connect with the narrow gauge line. This 10km 75cm gauge line closed on 1st January 1968. (D.Trevor Rowe).

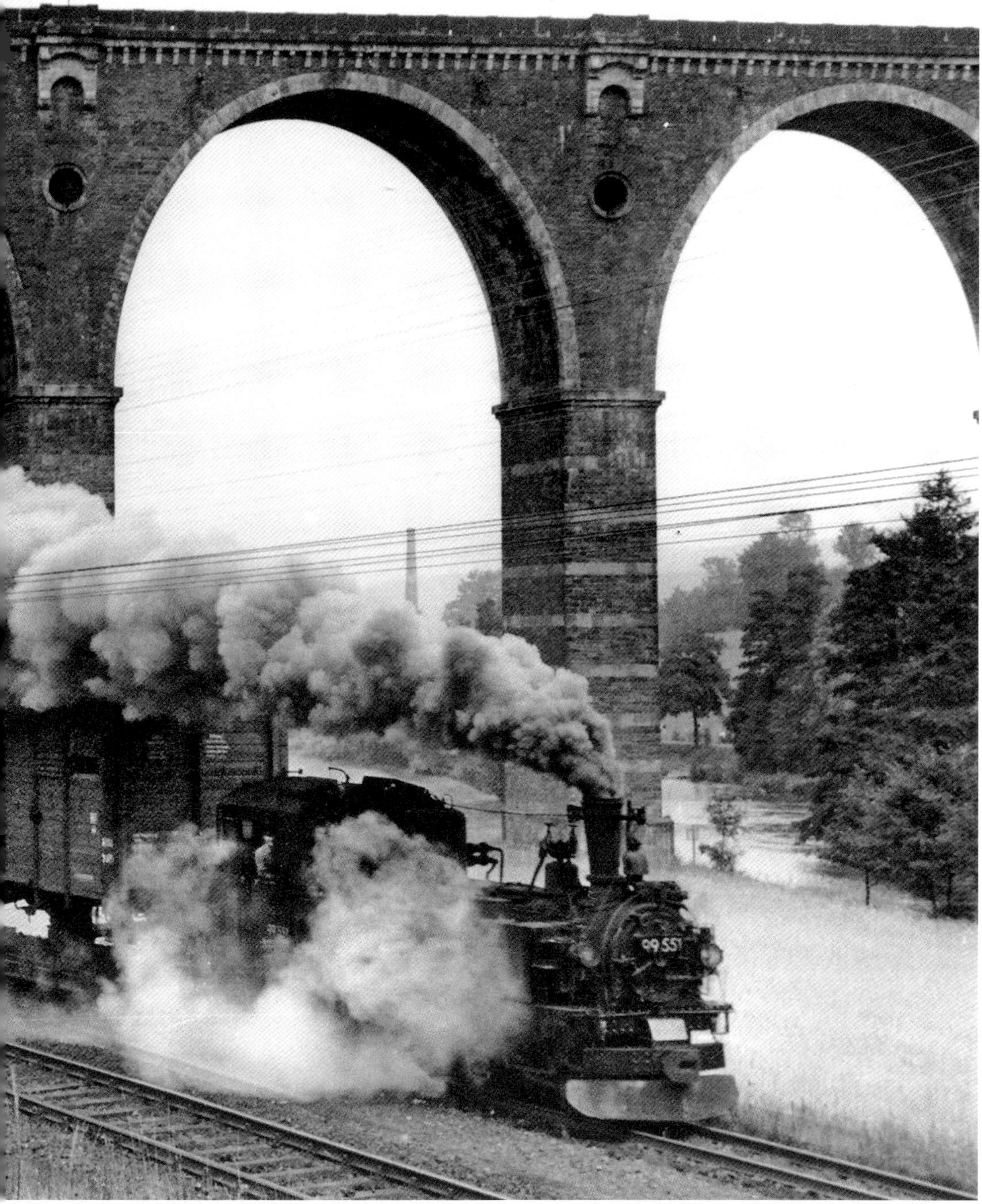
99 551

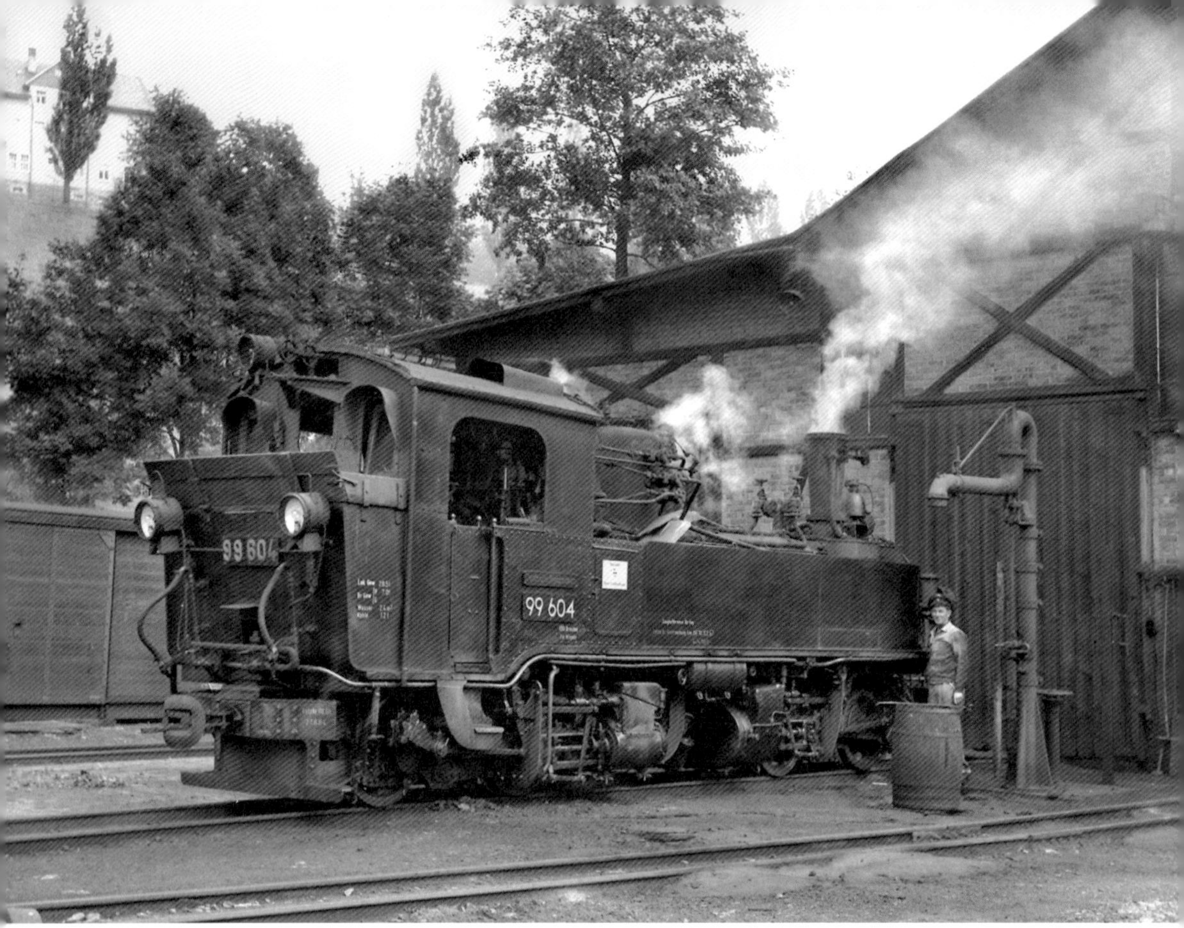
99 604
99 604

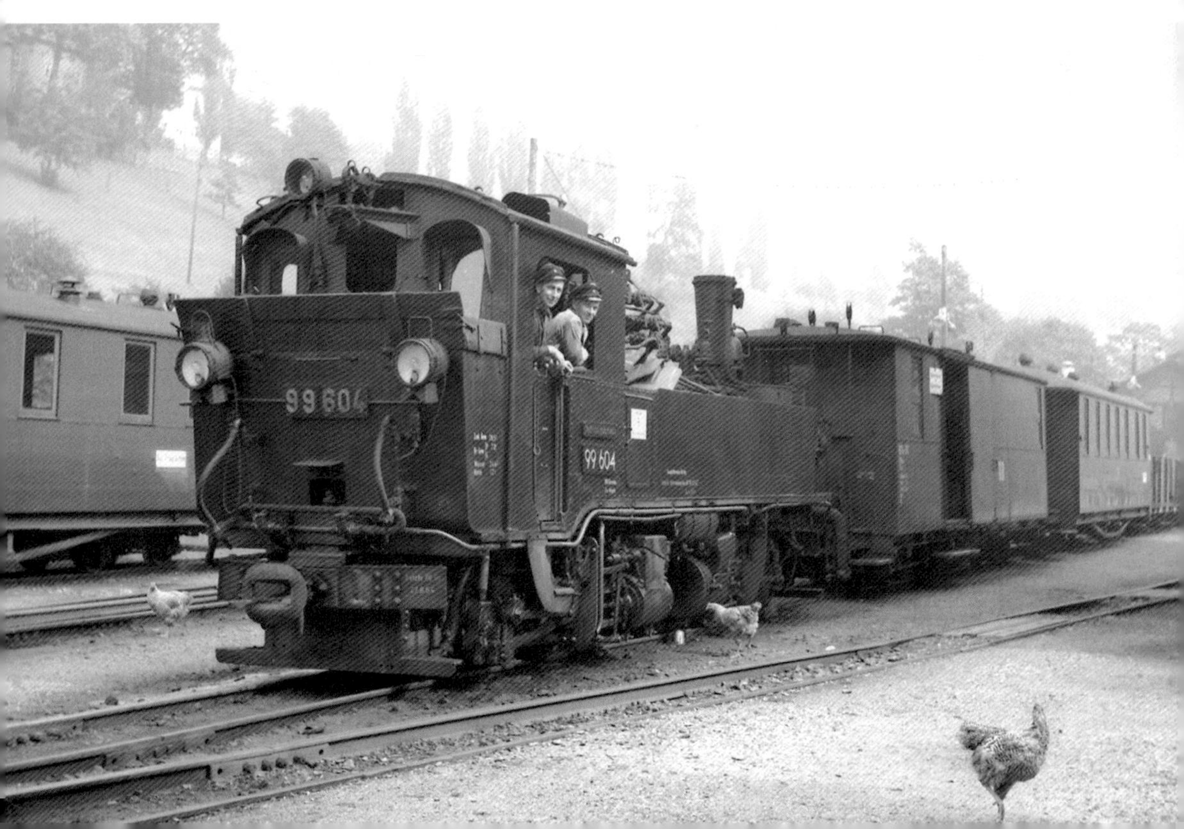
99 604
99 604

1.8. Meyer no. 99 604 is at rest outside the shed at Oberrittersgrün in August 1967. This line closed in 1971, however the station and depot complex has been preserved as a lasting reminder of the many similar lines in Saxony. (T.Martin).

1.9. The crew of the Meyer enjoyed having their photographs taken whilst the chicken population of Oberrittersgrün searched the ballast for food! (T.Martin).

1.10. Saxon-Meyer no. 99 599 was preparing to run around its train at Wolkenstein on the scenic line to Jöhstadt on 10th August 1963. Although this route closed in 1986, the upper section has been restored as a museum line known as the Pressnitztalbahn. (D.Trevor Rowe).

1.11. Meyer no. 99 1582-8 was recorded crossing the river Pressnitz on the approach to Steinbach whilst hauling a train between Wolkenstein and Jöhstadt on 22nd May 1983. This locomotive has been preserved and now operates on the museum line at Schönheide. (D.Trevor Rowe).

1.12. Another locomotive currently based at Schönheide is Meyer no. 99 1585-1 which was recorded at Steinbach with a train from Wolkenstein on 22nd May 1983. (D.Trevor Rowe).

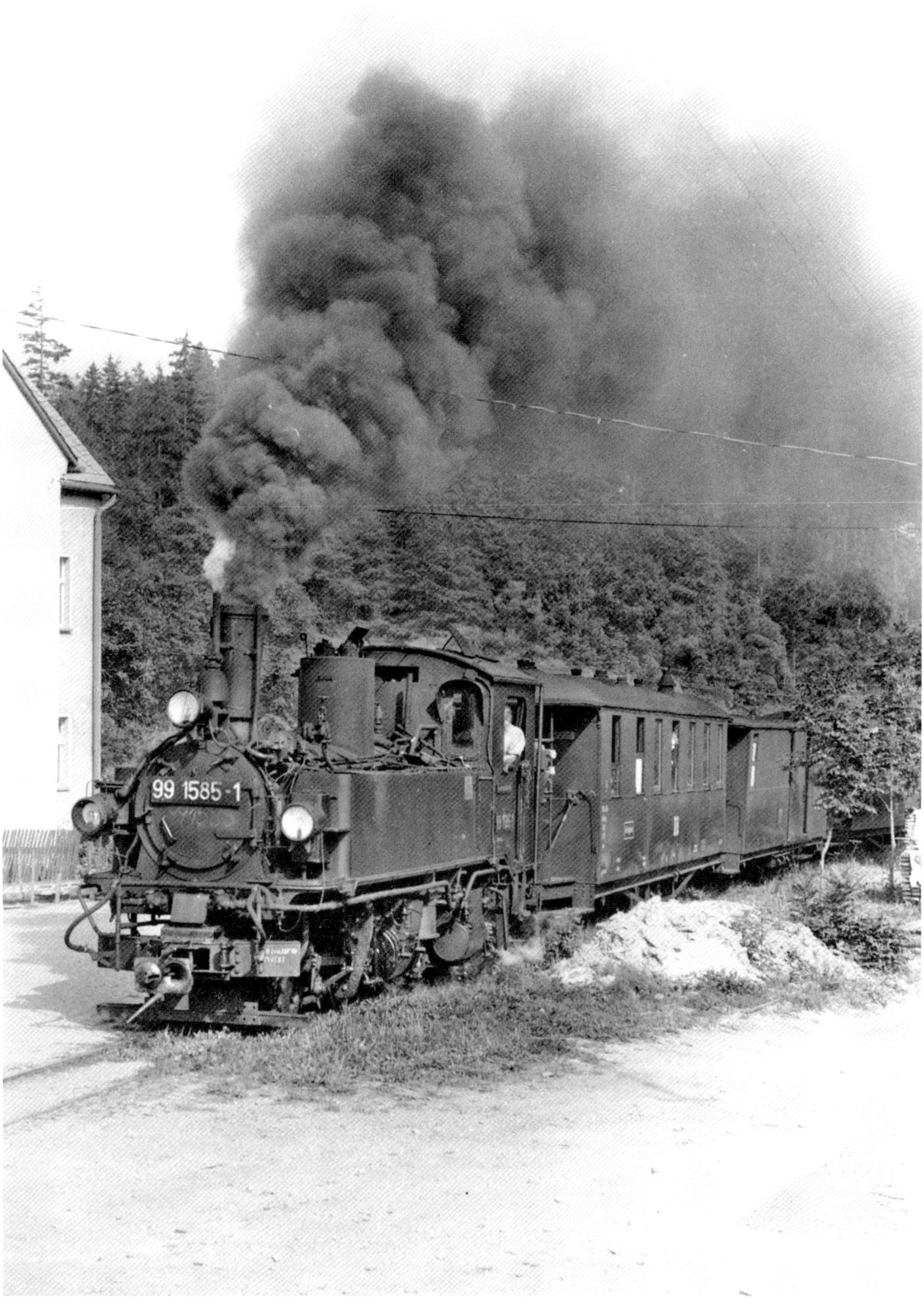
99 1585-1

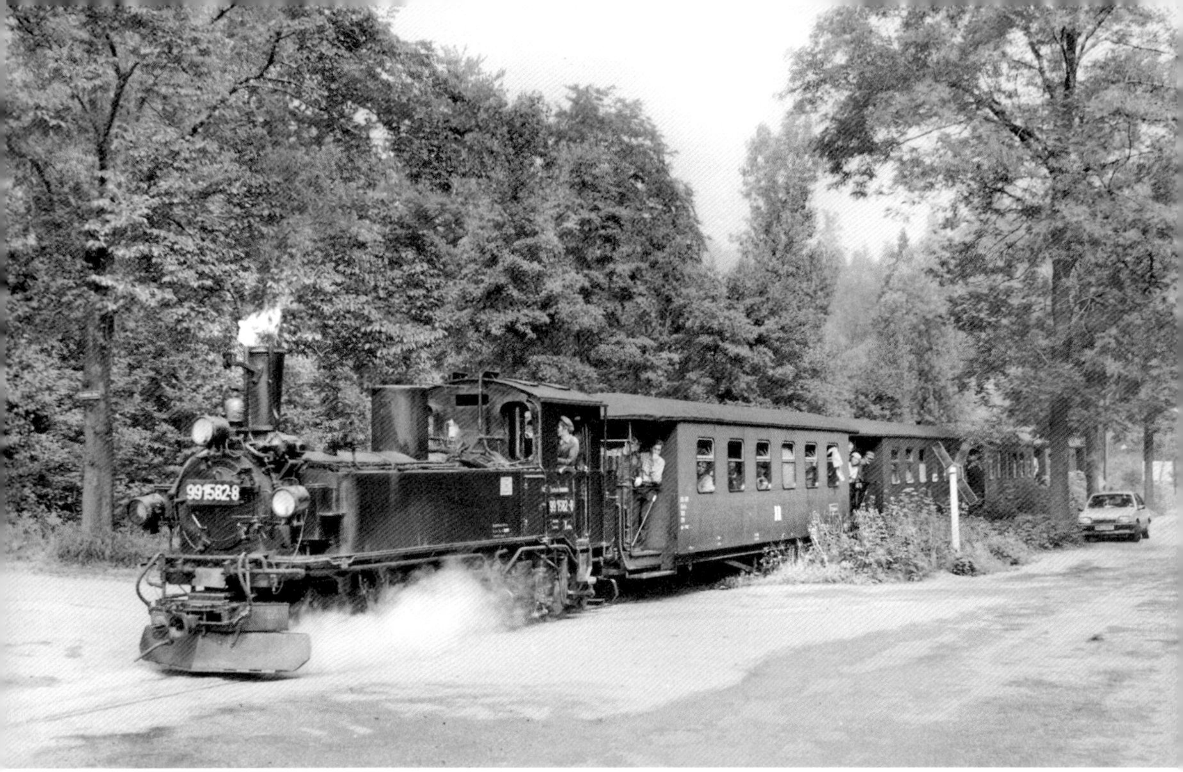
99 1582-8

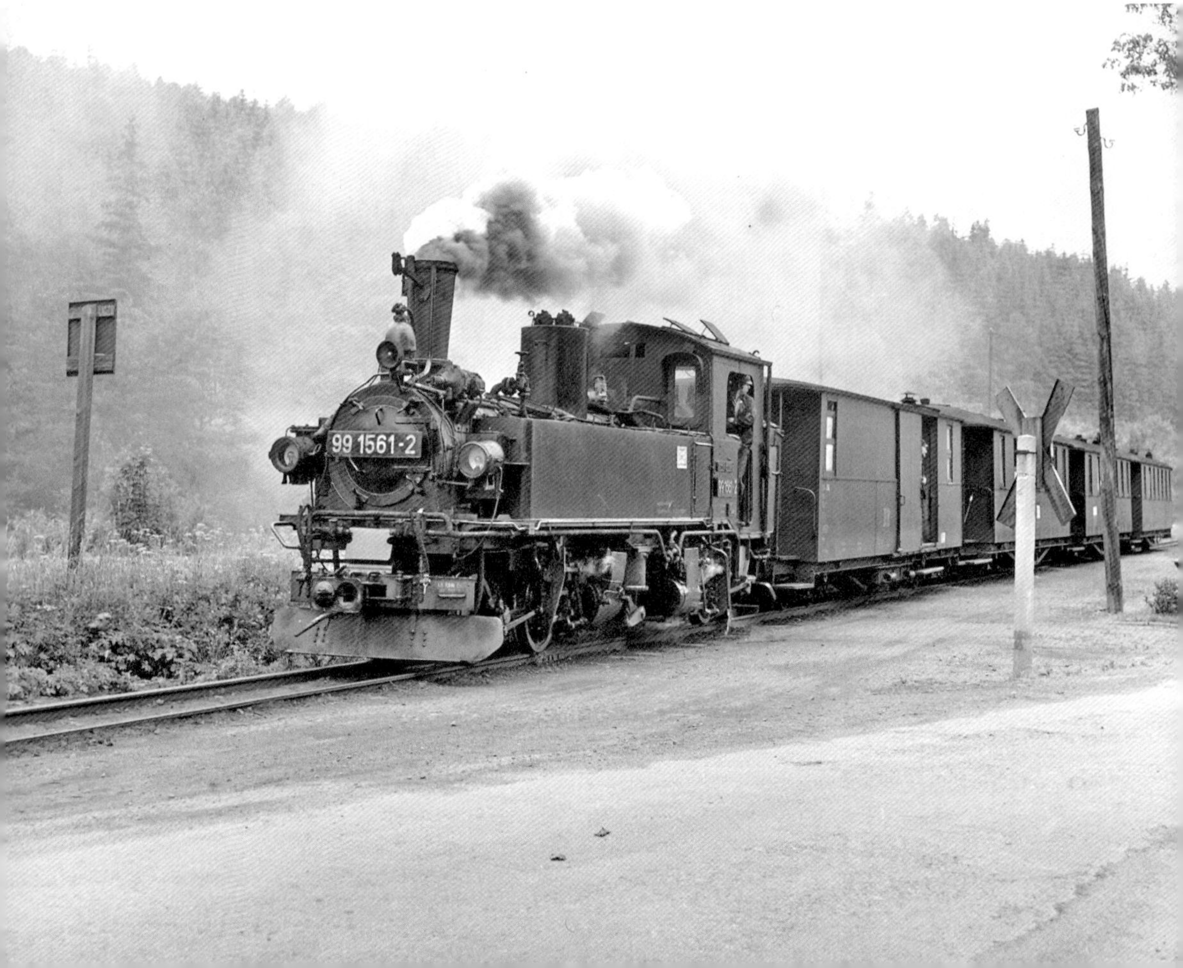
99 1561-2

1.13. Shortly after leaving Steinbach, the line passes this delightful roadside section before ascending the steep climb through the valley to Jöhstadt. With drain cocks open, no.99 1582-8 crossed the unprotected level crossing before attacking the gradient on 22nd May 1983. (D.Trevor Rowe).

1.14. Saxon-Meyers remained the only type of motive power employed for the majority of the Wolkenstein lines existence. Here no 99 1561-2 was viewed departing from Schlössel with an early morning passenger train on 5th July 1978. (B.Benn).

1.15. Meyer no. 99 1606-5 arrives at Jöhstadt, with a mixed train on 17th September 1981. During this period when the citizens of the GDR were enduring severe austerity, these minor branch lines were a lifeline to the rural communities – car ownership being restricted to the privileged few. (K.Taylorson).

1.16. The delightful depot at Jöhstadt, where two 0-4-4-0T Meyers were receiving maintenance was recorded in August 1967. No. 99 568 had in fact suffered bearing problems on its leading bogie during the journey from Wolkenstein. Consequently no. 99 596 was rapidly prepared for service in order to work the return train. (T.Martin).

1.17. Two Henschel Class VIK 0-10-0Ts, nos 99 642 and 99 653, stand outside the depot at Wilsdruff in August 1967. Along side the locomotives some very primitive depot equipment was dumped among the weeds. Most of the V1Ks were based at Wilsdruff during their final years of service. (T.Martin).

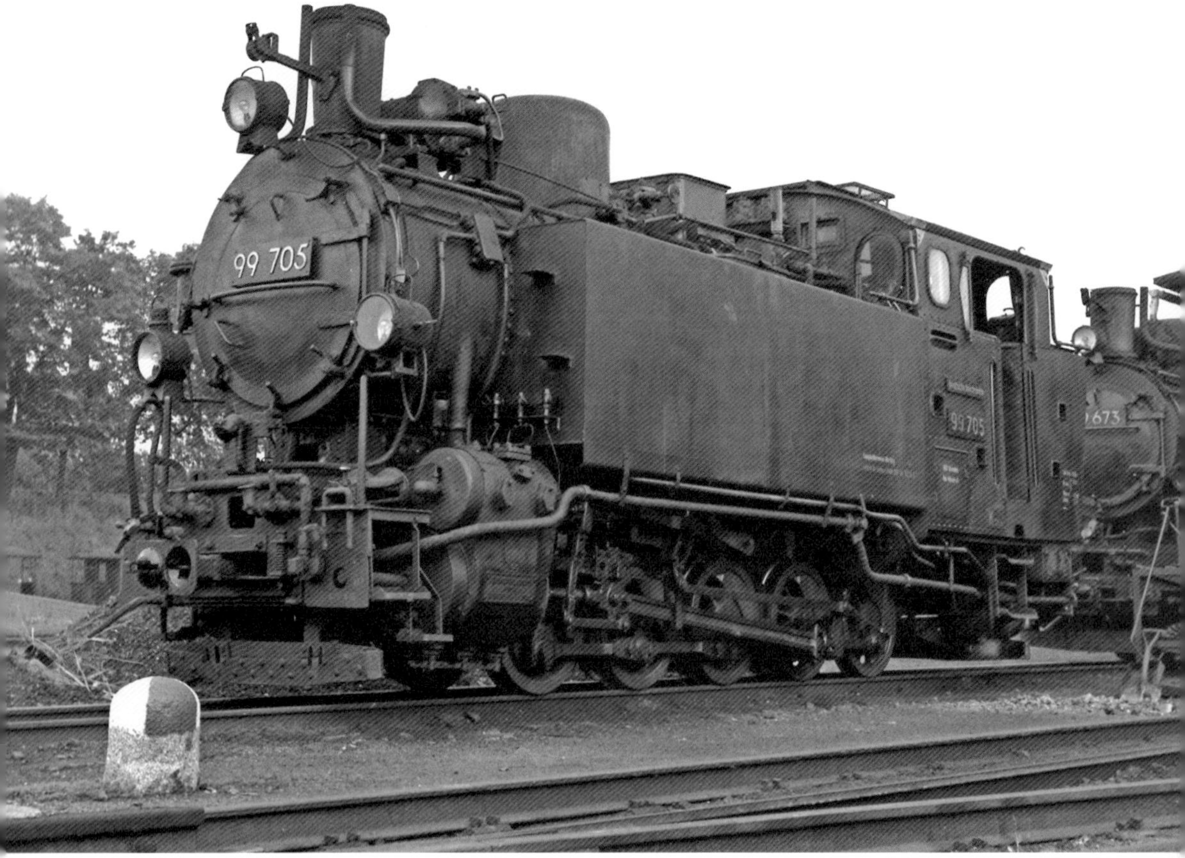
99 705
99 705

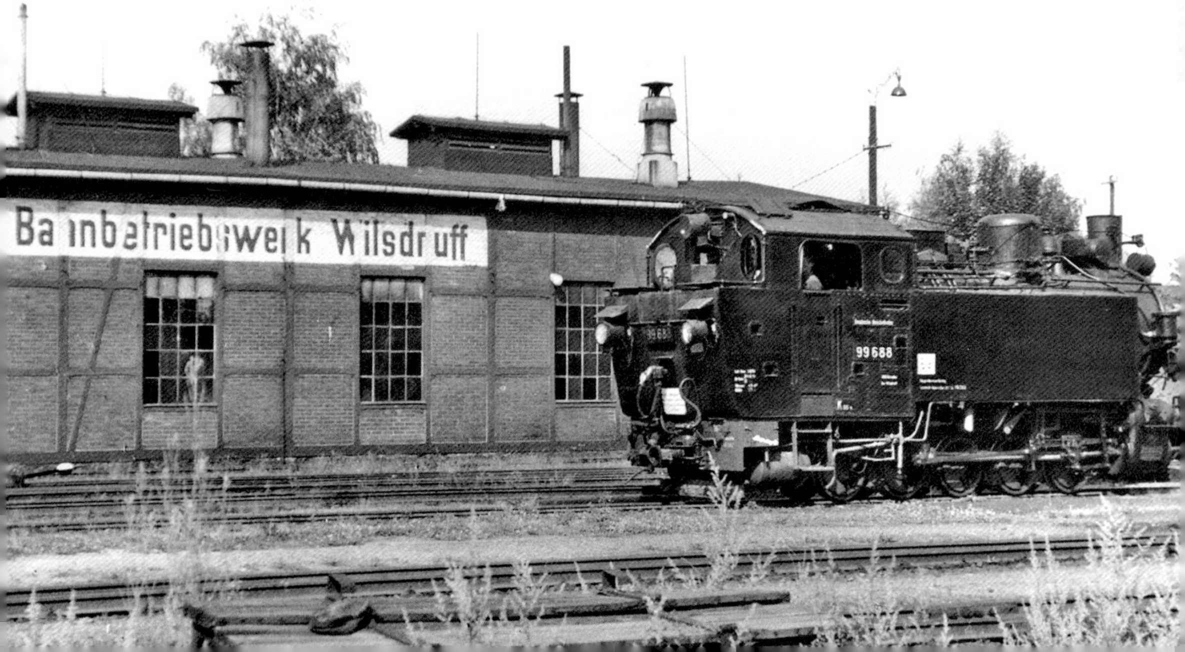
Ba nbetriebswe k Wilsdruff
99 688

1.18. Another Class V1K posed at Wilsdruff on the same occasion. No. 99 705 was one of the later examples built by M-G. Karlsruhe, in 1926. Shortly after these views were obtained, the photographer was arrested and his subsequent film destroyed. Such were the hazards encountered in the GDR during the "cold war" period. (T.Martin).

1.19. 0-10-0T no. 99 688 is passing the depot at Wilsdruff before collecting its train from the sidings on 6th August 1963. The majority of traffic at this location was comprised of freight trains between the various inter-linked lines of the Wilsdruff network. (D.Trevor Rowe).

1.20. No.99 688 waits to depart from Wilsdruff freight depot having collected its train including the obligatory standard gauge van on a rollwagen transporter. (D.Trevor Rowe).

1.21. No.99 689, another Class V1K 0-10-0T, leaves Freital-Potschappel on the dual gauge section leading to Freital-Hainsberg with a passenger train on 5th August 1963. Although the standard gauge rail has been removed, the 75cm track is still in place but it had seen very little traffic since the Wilsdruff network was closed in 1972. (D.Trevor Rowe).

1.22. The Saxon Narrow Gauge personified. Meyer no. 99 535 was recorded drifting through the woods near Lossnitz whilst hauling a mixed train from Eppendorf to Hetzdorf in August 1967. This Meyer was one of the original unrebuilt locomotives and is now preserved in Dresden Transport Museum. (T.Martin).

2. Saxon Narrow Gauge Locomotive Development

When construction of the first 75cm lines by the Saxon State Railways began, a modest 0-6-0T locomotive was deemed sufficient for their requirements. Ultimately 44 machines of this design were produced by Richard Hartmann at Chemnitz between 1881 and 1892, the last survivor not being withdrawn until 1964. In addition, a single 0-4-0T version was built for use during construction of the early lines. Known as the type 1K, these relatively small locomotives proved adequate for the initial services on the short isolated routes with their modest traffic requirements.

As the systems developed and traffic increased, a need for more powerful locomotives was found to be necessary. In 1885 two 0-4-4-0T "Fairlie" locomotives were supplied from England by Hawthorn of Newcastle. Known as type 11K alt, they had a fairly short life in Saxony and were withdrawn by 1910. Unperturbed by the apparent lack of success of these articulated locomotives, two 0-6-6-0Ts were constructed locally in 1913. Known as type 11K neu, they were in fact the result of uniting the first four 1Ks "back to back" into rigid double engines known as Zwillinge (twins). These proved to be no more successful than the Hawthorn "Fairlies", both being withdrawn by 1926.

As the quest for more powerful locomotives continued, another semi-articulated design was accepted. This took the form of an 0-6-2T with its driving axles articulated on the Klose system, which incorporated intricate gears on the axle boxes. Known as type 111K, six of these complex machines were supplied by Krauss and Hartmann between 1889 and 1891. Obviously the complexities of the geared axles proved too much; these locomotives were also withdrawn in 1926.

Whilst all the experiments with various articulated and double engines were being carried out, Sächsische Maschinenfabrik (SMF), formerly Richard Hartmann, at Chemnitz produced in 1892 the prototype of a locomotive that was to become synonymous with the narrow gauge lines of Saxony. This became the class 1VK 0-4-4-0T Meyer design, known as the legendary type K44 Saxon-Meyer. A total of 96 of these very successful machines was built between 1892 and 1921 of which 22 have survived to date, although not all are in working order. Equally at home hauling standard gauge freight wagons on rollwagens or passenger trains, these venerable compound locomotives have earned their place in railway history as one of the most successful narrow gauge designs. With their long low slung boilers, low pressure cylinders on the rear of the front bogie unit and high pressure to the front of the rear units, they had a definite purposeful appearance matched by their excellent performance. Such was their success that during the 1960s, 25 of the class received comprehensive rebuilds to the extent that they were considered to be new locomotives from an accountancy point of view! Not surprisingly, the majority of the surviving examples of these illustrious machines are from this batch of reconstructed locomotives.

Despite the undoubted success of the 1VK Meyers, the need for an even more powerful design was required. Between 1901 and 1908 SMF Hartmann supplied a class of nine 0-8-0Ts for heavy freight haulage. Known as the class VK, these proved reasonably successful, the last of the type surviving in service until 1942. However they were to be eclipsed by a design that owes its origin to the First World War. During the latter years of the conflict, a successful 0-10-0T was supplied to the Heeresfeldbahn military railways. Like the ubiquitous 0-8-0T "Feldbahn" 60cm locomotives used prolifically by the German Army, these larger machines were constructed to a common design by a variety of manufacturers. 15 examples built by Henschel, M-G Karlsruhe and SMF Hartmann were transferred to the Saxon State Railways following the end of hostilities in 1918. Known as The class V1K, they were joined by a further 47 locomotives of the same design supplied to Deutsche Reichsbahn-Gesellschaft between 1923 and 1927, DRG having taken control of the Saxon railways in 1920. Of this large class of superheated 0-10-0Ts, which in later years were largely based at Wilsdruff, only four have survived of which two are still at work in Saxony.

Following the delivery of the last of the 0-10-0Ts in 1927, the combined talents of SMF Hartmann at Chemnitz and Schwartzkopff at Berlin produced an improved version, having proved with the V1Ks that a ten coupled design was quite suitable for use on a 75cm gauge system. The new locomotives were the illustrious V11K alt 2-10-2Ts of which 32 were built between 1928 and 1933. Such was the success of this design, a further 24 were built between 1952 and 1956 by VEB Locomotivbrau "Karl Marx" at Babelsberg (LKM). Known as type V11K neu, these later locomotives incorporated many of the features used in the metre gauge machines supplied by LKM for use on the Harz system during the same period. Of the original 32 locomotives, 14 have survived to date whilst all but two of the later machines are still in service. As with the metre gauge 2-10-2Ts, both variants of the V11Ks are fitted with a multitude of domes and associated pipes together with air brake compressors and electric generators. In common with the class 1VK Meyers, the two variants of V11K 2-10-2Ts have become indelibly associated with the Saxon narrow gauge lines. However, in recent years five of the later version have migrated to other parts of Germany whilst in 1956 LKM also supplied 15 examples for use in Bulgaria. The LKM locomotives are among the most powerful 75cm gauge locomotives in Europe. With a weight in working order of 58 tonnes and a power rating of 565hp, they are more than equal to the tasks demanded of them. The official name for the 2-10-2Ts was K57 Einheitsloks although the more familiar unofficial V11K is normally used to describe them.

The accompanying photographs will show a wide range of numbering variations, as a result of changes of ownership of the Saxon lines since 1881. The earliest locomotives carried Saxon State Railway numbers, simply nos 1 to 224 and were painted green. From 1920 ownership changed to DRG and in 1925 a renumbering scheme was introduced. This featured a 99 prefix followed by a three digit running number. Hence a Meyer originally numbered 132 became 99 539. At the same period, the livery changed to the familiar black with red frames and motion. The numbers carried by the locomotives remained the same after DRG ownership was transferred to DR in 1945. In 1970 DR introduced its new numbering scheme, which added 1xxx to the running number and a suffix for computerisation records. Thus 99 582 became 99 1582-8, the suffix numbers having no logical sequence as in the case of the Harz locomotives. Following the amalgamation with DB in 1992, another far more drastic renumbering took place. The 99 prefix was replaced by a 099 prefix, followed by a three digit running number and the computer suffix. The running numbers bore no resemblance to the original numbers, which made identification of individual locomotives difficult to trace. As an example of these, no. 99 788 (later 99 1788-8) became 099 752-8 under the DB numbering system. Since the privatisation of the surviving lines, the locomotives have reverted to DR numbers of either pre or post 1970 schemes.

The earlier locomotives constructed for the Saxon State Railways were fitted with a very basic cable braking system. Known as the Heberlein system, this comprised a cable running between the front and rear buffer beams via pulleys attached to the chimney and cab roof. This was connected to a similar cable system that ran over the top of the freight wagons or coaches. The Meyers were the last locomotives to be fitted with these brakes, some of the surviving machines having retained the equipment for demonstration purposes. During the DRG period of operation, this very crude system was replaced initially by vacuum and ultimately air braking systems. However some of the short isolated branches, such as that between Hetzdorf and Grosswaltersdorf, continued to use Heberlein brakes until they were closed during the 1960s.

Although each of the individual lines possessed workshop facilities, major locomotive repairs and overhauls were carried out at one of the DR works. Until reunification, the majority of the work was carried out at Görlitz Works, situated at the most easterly town in Germany, close by the Polish border. During the last decade and the transfer of the workshops to DB ownership, much of the work has been carried out at Meiningen Works in the southwest of the old GDR, near to the border with the former West Germany. With so many of the narrow gauge lines being transferred to the private sector during the recent past, many overhauls are now carried out at the privately owned works at Kloster Mansfeld near Halle. These large workshops are fully equipped to carry out all manner of maintenance for steam locomotives. Some of the work carried out at Görlitz during the final years of DR ownership was so extensive that the locomotives emerged as virtually new machines.

2.1. Following a short period evaluating the merits of various designs of locomotives, which included Fairlies and 0-6-2Ts with Klose articulation, the most successful locomotives supplied to the Saxon State Railways were the Hartmann Class 1VK 0-4-4-0T Saxon-Meyers. The first of these remarkable machines was delivered in 1892 and construction continued until 1921 with a total of 96 locomotives produced. One of the preserved "new build" Meyers, no. 99 1542-2, was seen in immaculate condition at Steinbach on the Pressnitztalbahn on 20th May 2004. (J.F.Organ).

Deutsche Reichsbahn
994532-0
K44

Deutsche Reichsbahn
99 705

2.2.   Although none of the Saxon Class VK 0-8-0Ts has survived, a similar locomotive built by Orenstein & Koppel in 1908 for the Trusetalbahn in Thüringen has been based at Zittau since 1962. This interesting locomotive was recorded at Zittau Hbf on 25th August 1983, during one of the occasional visits from its normal base at Bertsdorf. (D.Trevor Rowe).

2.3.   The class V1K 0-10-0Ts had a very "chunky" appearance due to their relatively short length. No. 99 705 built by M.G.Karlsruhe in1926 was recorded at Wilsdruff depot in August 1967. Sadly only four of these excellent machines have survived, of which two are in Saxony. (T.Martin).

2.4.   Framed against the skeletal remains of the roof canopies at Dippoldiswalde, Schwartzkopff-built 2-10-2T Class V11K alt no. 099 734-6 (DR no.99 1761-8) was resting between duties on 3rd August 1992. The feed water heating equipment fitted to the earlier V11Ks is clearly shown in this view. (B.Benn).

2.5. Last of the line. The final V11K neu 2-10-2T built by LKM in 1956, no. 99 794, was recorded outside the new depot and workshop at Oberwiesenthal on 18th May 2004. The locomotive had recently returned to traffic following an extensive overhaul and was immaculately presented. Note the absence of the feed water equipment and resultant cleaner lines of the LKM machines. (J.F.Organ).

Freital Hainsberg- Kurort Kipsdorf

Freital Hainsberg
Cossmannsdorf
Rabenau
Spechtritz
Seifersdorf
Malter
Dippoldiswalde
Ulberndorf
Obercarsdorf
Schmiedeberg-Naundorf
Schmiedeberg
Buschmühle
Kurort Kipsdorf

Narrow Gauge
Standard Gauge

3. Freital Hainsberg to Kurort Kipsdorf

This 26.66km line was opened in two stages during 1882 and 1883. Initially the 22.25km from Freital Hainsberg, south west of Dresden, to Schmiedeberg being completed followed by the final 4.41km to the southern terminus the following year. Freital Hainsberg is situated on the main line between Dresden and Chemnitz, 10km from Dresden city centre, whilst Kurort Kipsdorf is a spa town 533m high in the eastern extremity of the mountain chain. The two termini were linked by a line of great scenic charm with many contrasts, which maintained both an extensive passenger and freight service until the latter ceased to operate in 1996. In 1913 a 3.25km dual gauge connecting line was opened between Freital Hainsberg and Freital Potschappel which linked the Kipsdorf line with the Wilsdruff network.

Leaving the station at Freital Hainsberg, adjacent to the standard gauge route, the line drops down an incline in order to pass under the main line before proceeding south to Cossmannsdorf. Within a short distance, the 75cm tracks enter the dramatic scenery of the Rabenau Gorge where the railway and River Weisseritz are in close proximity. The initial part of this section originally passed through a tunnel, which was opened into a deep cutting following the introduction of standard gauge freight wagons on transporters in 1905. After leaving the section through the gorge, Seifersdorf is the next intermediate station following which the line then passes over a viaduct, crossing a corner of the reservoir near Malter, followed by an area of pastoral countryside.

The important intermediate station at Dippoldiswalde, approximately half way along the route, has many sidings where much of the freight traffic was delivered. It is also the principal passing point on the line where locomotives heading for Kurort Kipsdorf clean their fires and take on water. After leaving Dippoldiswalde the route adopts a roadside location before the climb towards the mountains and the original temporary terminus at Schmiedeberg. Shortly before the latter town is reached, the line passes a siding that leads into a scrap yard buried among the trees. This was the source of the final freight traffic until the yard was closed in 1996. Leaving Schmiedeberg, the line crosses a 191m long curved viaduct that passes 10m above the rooftops of the town. There then follows the long 1 in 33 gradient to the upper terminus at Kurort Kipsdorf, passing a busy level crossing on the final part of the climb. The station layout was originally quite extensive with a total of seven platform roads, although this has been simplified in more recent years.

The Kipsdorf line continued to provide a regular passenger and freight service into the post-reunification period. With DB wishing to close or sell its remaining narrow gauge lines during the 1990s, it was obvious that the line was continuing to operate with a huge question mark over its future. With the cessation of freight traffic in 1996, the future looked even more insecure and the prospect of it being sold to a private operator appeared to be the only option by the end of the 20th century. Amazingly DB continued to operate a reduced passenger service under the title of Weisseritztalbahn for a further six years until the catastrophic floods that struck Eastern Europe in August 2002 sealed the lines fate. Much of the route through the Rabenau Gorge and the upper section beyond Schmiedeberg was washed away by the swollen river and will require a completely new alignment if it is rebuilt. One locomotive and its rolling stock became marooned at Dippoldiswalde, the remaining eight 2-10-2Ts and one Meyer were fortunately safely housed in the depot at Freital, along with the rolling stock.

However, steam operations continued on some undamaged sections of the line such as that between Freital Potschappel and Freital Cossmannsdorf. From February 2004, Meyer no. 99 1564 has operated passenger trains between Seifersdorf and Dippoldiswalde assisted by the recently restored class V1K 0-10-0T no. 99 715. During the period of closure, in addition to these special workings, the station roof at Dippoldiswalde removed by DR has recently been restored by the preservation group, which is based at the station.

3.1.   0-4-4-0T Saxon-Meyers, nos 99 1590 and 99 1608, stand at Freital-Hainsberg depot prior to hauling a special charter mixed train to Kurort-Kipsdorf in October 1994. The leading locomotive was paying a visit from Jöhstadt, in order to join the home based Meyer for the occasion. (B.Benn).

3.2.   Class V11K alt 2-10-2T no. 99 743 passes through the yard at Freital-Hainsberg before hauling a train to Kipsdorf on 5th August 1963. Photography at such a busy railway centre during that period was extremely hazardous, being frowned upon by the authorities. (D.Trevor Rowe).

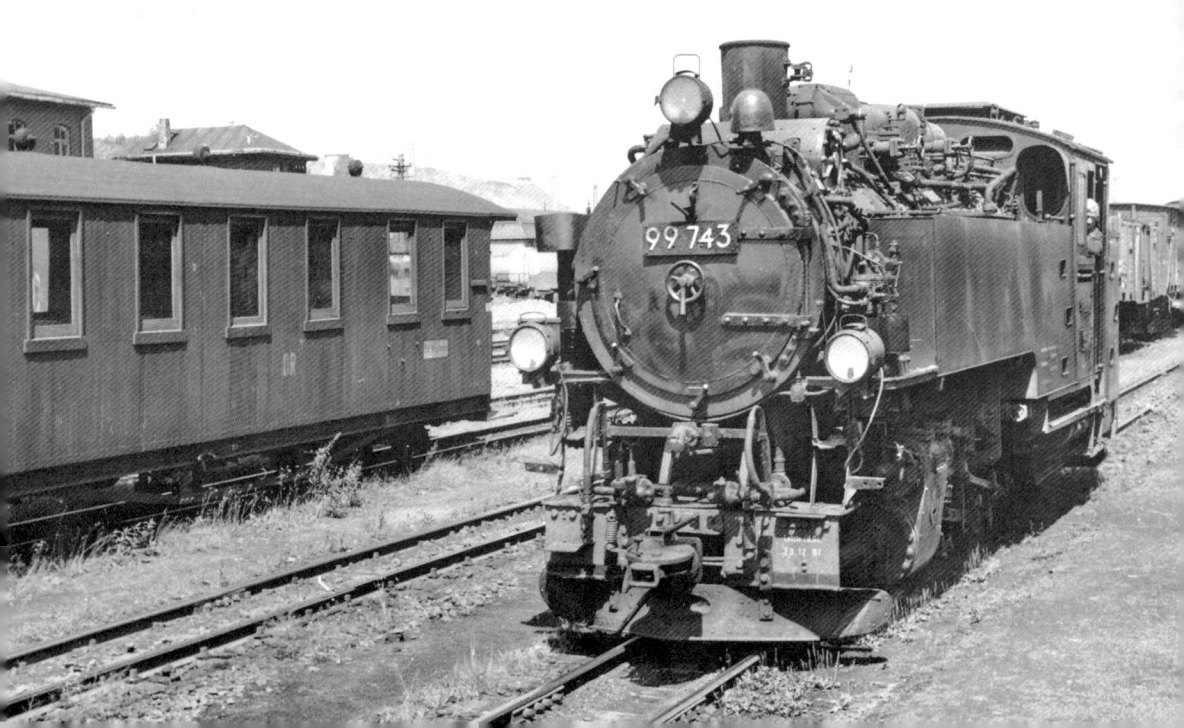

3.3. During the early period of DB operation following reunification, Class V11K neu 2-10-2T no.099 736-1 (DR no.99 771) was recorded accelerating away from Freital-Hainsberg with the afternoon coal train bound for Dippoldiswalde on 4th August 1992. (Mrs.B.Benn).

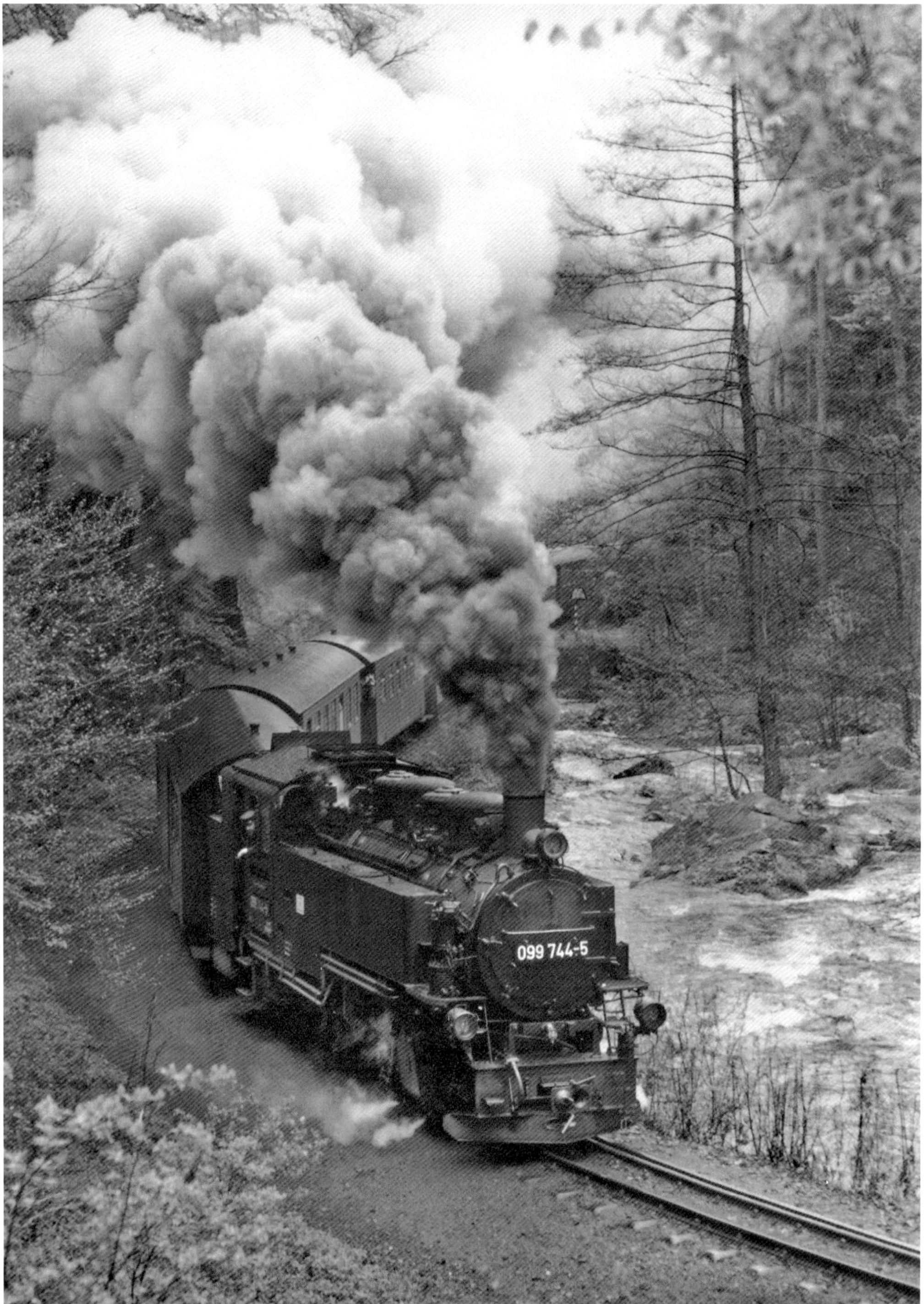
099 744-5

3.4. Another Class V11K neu 2-10-2T, with its DB number 099-744-5 (DR no.99 780), was heading through the Rabenau Gorge with a passenger train from Freital-Hainsberg to Kurort Kipsdorf on 2nd May 1992. This section of the line was seriously damaged during the severe floods that struck the area in August 2002. (B.Benn).

3.5. 2-10-2T no. 099-736-1 drifts down through the Rabenau Gorge with a Freital bound passenger train on 12th August 1992. Hopefully this highly scenic stretch of line will be rebuilt in the not too distant future. (B.Benn).

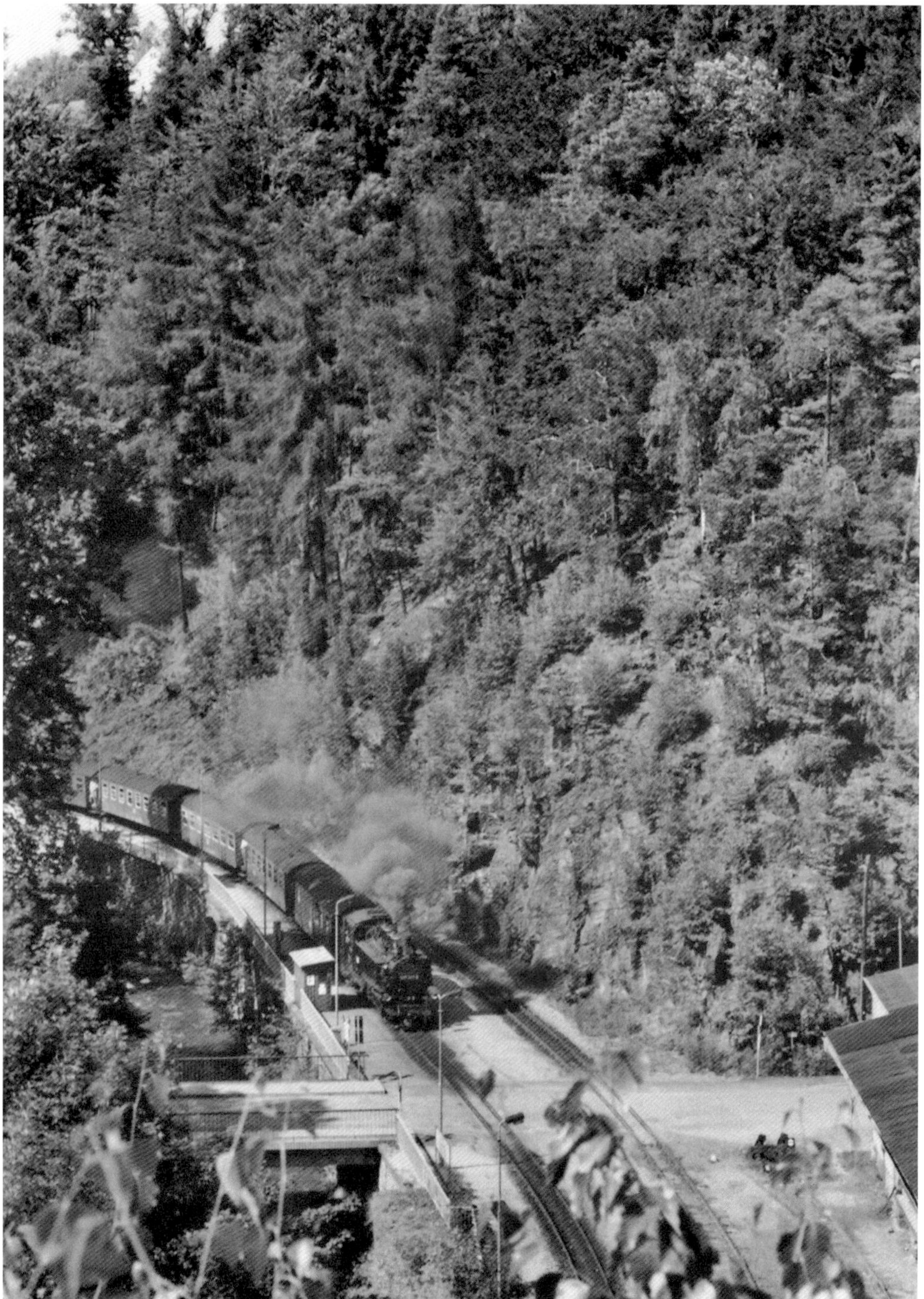

3.6. An indication of the delightful scenic splendour of the Rabenau Gorge can be gained from this elevated view of Rabenau station, situated alongside the River Weisseritz, in August 1996. (B.Benn).

3.7. Class V11K alt 2-10-2T no. 099-726-2 (99 746) departing from Seifersdorf with a heavy coal train to Dippoldiswalde on 4th August 1992. Freight traffic was a regular feature of the Freital line until 1996. (B.Benn).

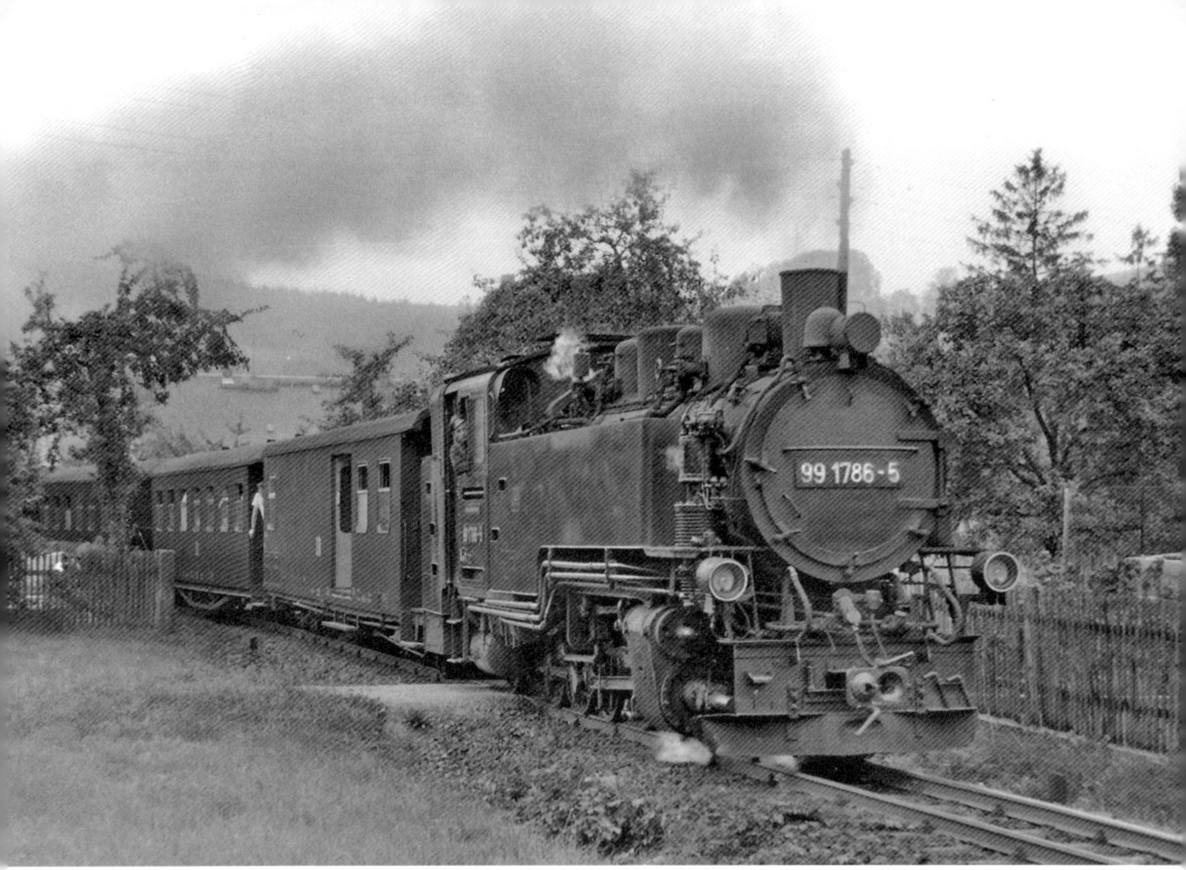
99 1786-5

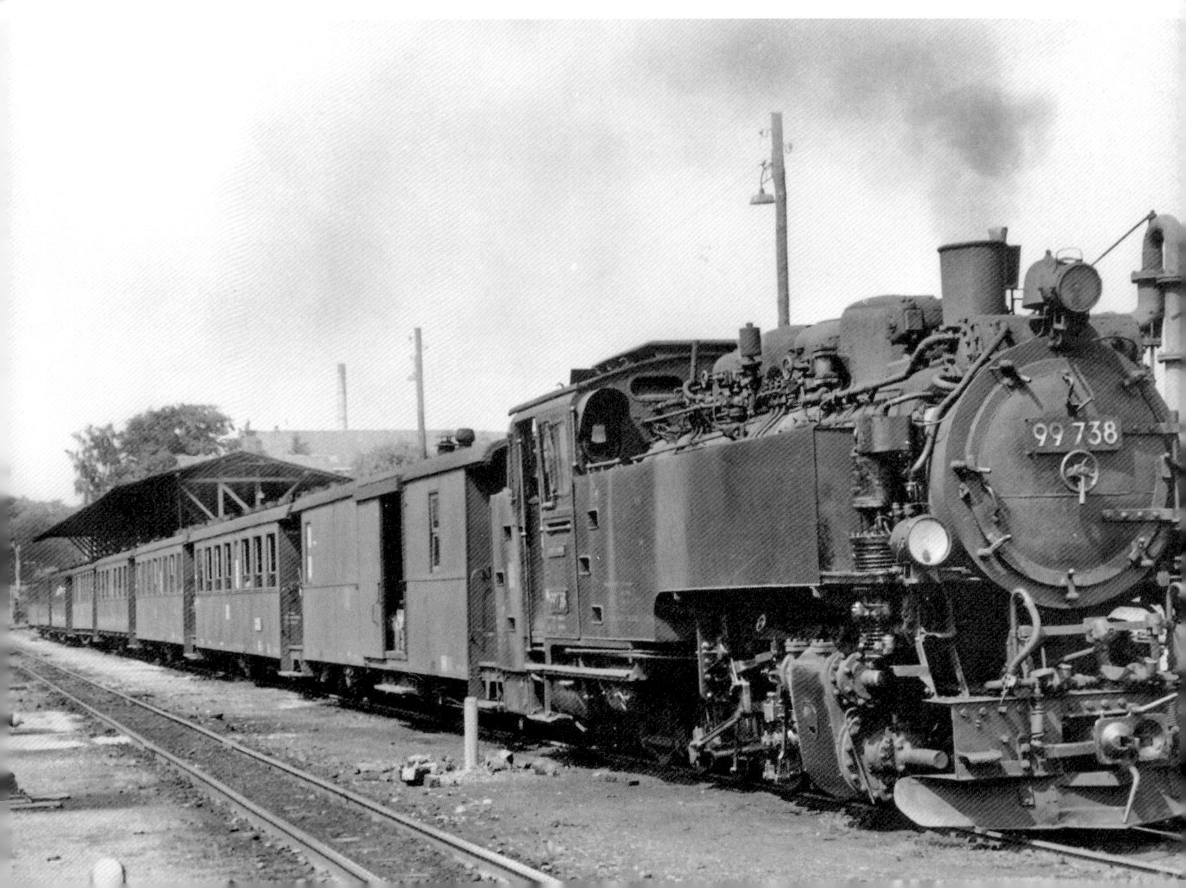
99 738

3.8. One of the LKM 2-10-2Ts, no. 99 1786-5 was recorded near Dippoldiswalde hauling a passenger train on 23rd August 1983. Note the rural charm of this section of the route. (D.Trevor Rowe).

3.9. Still carrying its old DR number 99 738, a Class V11K alt 2-10-2T is about to depart from Dippoldiswalde on 5th August 1963. At that time the station still retained the platform roof canopies protecting the waiting passengers from the elements. (D.Trevor Rowe).

3.10. Two Class V11K neu 2-10-2Ts were soon to depart from Dippoldiswalde with a Freital bound passenger train on 16th September 1981. The platform canopies, which were removed during the 1980s, have recently been replaced. (K.Taylorson).

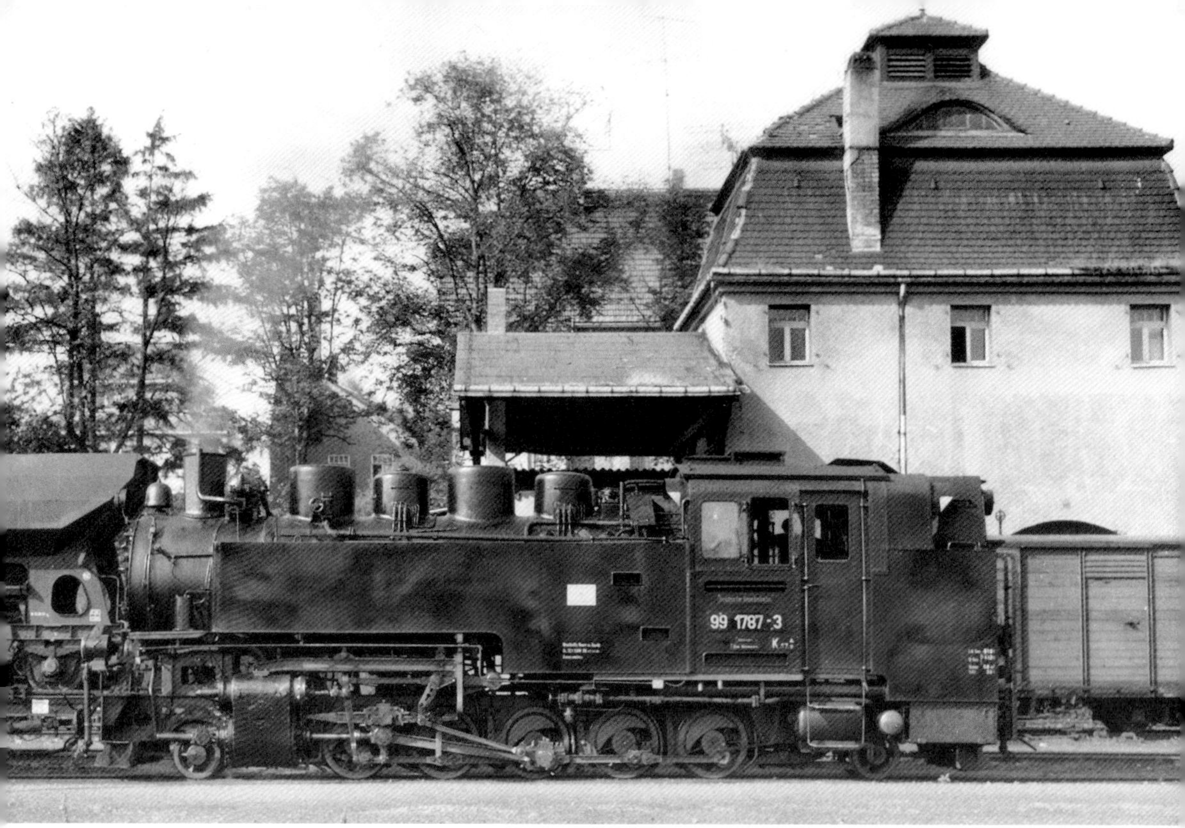
99 1787-3

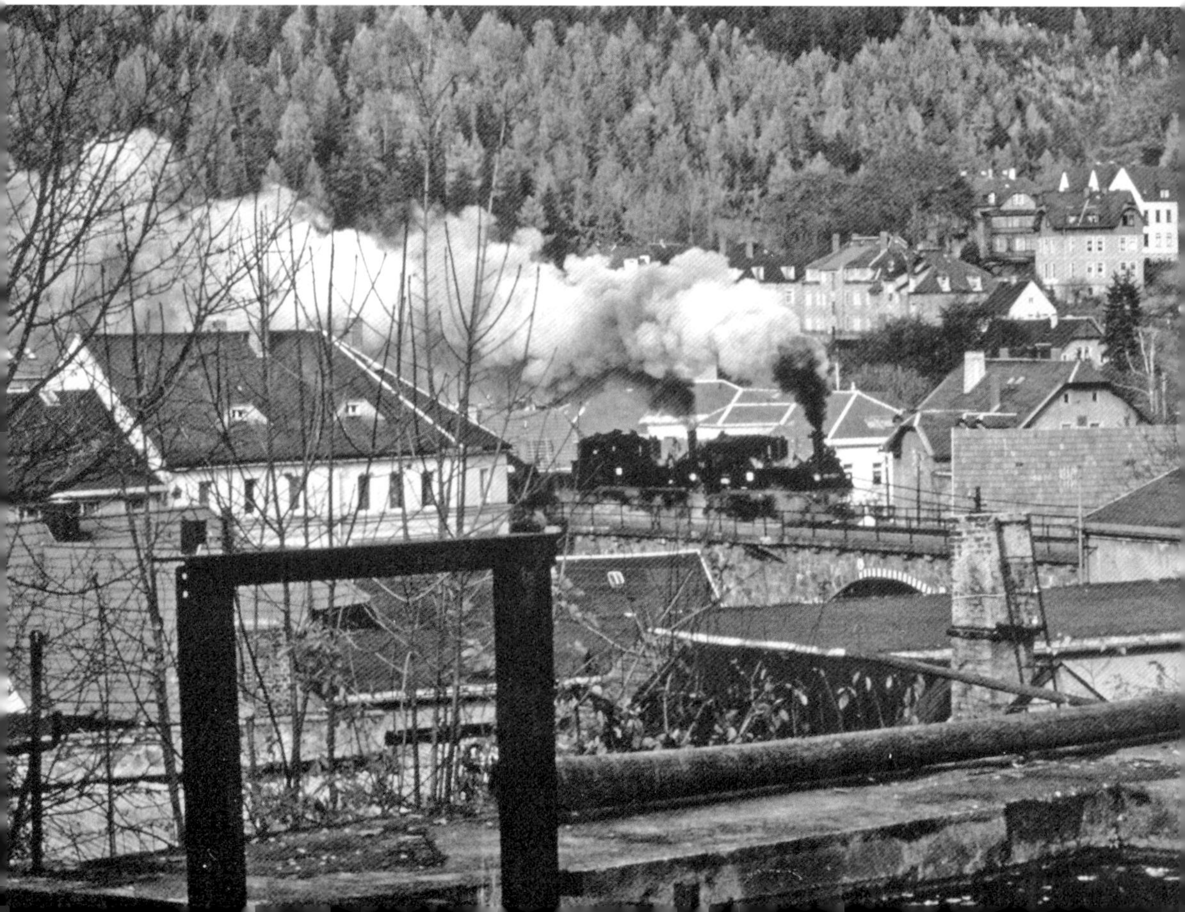

3.11. The small diameter of the driving wheels of these powerful 2-10-2Ts can be seen in this view of no.99 1787-3 standing in Dippoldiswalde station on 27th August 1990. (J.Wiseman).

3.12. On a beautiful autumn day in October 1994, 0-4-4-0T Saxon-Meyers nos. 99 1590 and 99 1608 hauled a special mixed train across the viaduct at Schmiedeberg. The close proximity of the rooftops to the viaduct can be seen in this view. (B.Benn).

3.13. With its original DR number 99 734 restored to the smokebox but retaining its DB number of 099-723-9 on the cab side, one of the earliest Class V11K alt 2-10-2Ts was viewed replenishing its water tanks upon arrival at Kurort Kipsdorf on 12th August 1996. (B.Benn).

4. Radebeul to Radeburg

Situated to the northwest of Dresden, this 16.55km line was opened in 1884 and has continued to provide a mainly commuter service since that time. Freight traffic of a mainly domestic nature was carried until 1991, whilst during the late 1930s there was a considerable amount of traffic in connection with the building of an autobahn in the vicinity.

The major terminus of this line is situated at Radebeul Ost where it shares an island platform with the Dresden suburban line to Meissen. The 75cm line proceeds in a northerly direction, initially running parallel to the standard gauge. The route then runs through the suburbs and shortly negotiates a busy level crossing of a main road at Weisses Ross incorporating the double tracks of the Dresden tramway system. More residential suburbs and sections of roadside running are encountered, overlooked by steep hillsides of extensive terraced vineyards, before passing through vast and attractive woodland. Following the two stations at Friedewald, the line crosses a causeway that separates two lakes until the major intermediate station at Moritzburg is reached, at the mid-way point of the route. Moritzburg is famed for its magnificent hunting palace and lake, a baroque extravaganza built in the 1720s on the site of an earlier castle built in 1542 by Duke Moritz of Saxony.

The remainder of the route to the upper terminus passes through an area of farmland and lakes, including another section of roadside running, with a maximum gradient of 1 in 60 on the final ascent to Radeburg. A three-road engine shed is located at Radeburg along with a number of sidings. In recent years this has become the home of some of the historic locomotives and rolling stock that have been preserved on the line. Normal operations are in the hands of the ubiquitous class V11K 2-10-2Ts, of which eight examples have been based at Radebeul in recent years.

The historic locomotives based at Radeburg include two class 1VK Meyers (99 539 and 99 1608) and one of the last surviving V1K 0-10-0Ts in Saxony (99 713). The earlier of the two Meyers has been restored to its original green livery and its Saxon State Railways number of 132. These are used for the haulage of traditionszüg trains that are operated on a regular basis by a supporting society known as Traditionsbahn Radebeul in co-operation with DB. A collection of vintage vacuum braked rolling stock has also been preserved by the society at Radeburg.

Since 1992, when control of the remaining Saxon narrow gauge lines was transferred from DR to DB, the new regime have maintained the service although more attuned to the tourist industry rather than as a commuter operation. A marketing title of Lössnitzgrundbahn was adopted during the late 1990s in an attempt to attract more patronage. However, as with all its other minor routes, DB were anxious to close or dispose of the line rather than incur additional expense on its upkeep. During early 2004 it was announced that the Lössnitzgrundbahn was soon to be taken over by BVO Bahn GmbH, a private bus company that already operates one of the other Saxon narrow gauge lines based at Oberwiesenthal. This transfer actually took place on 10th June 2004, the final train to be operated by DB being hauled by Meyer no. 99 1608 and 0-10-0T no.99 713. This occasion was historic in being the last train on any gauge of the DB network to be operated with vacuum braked stock.

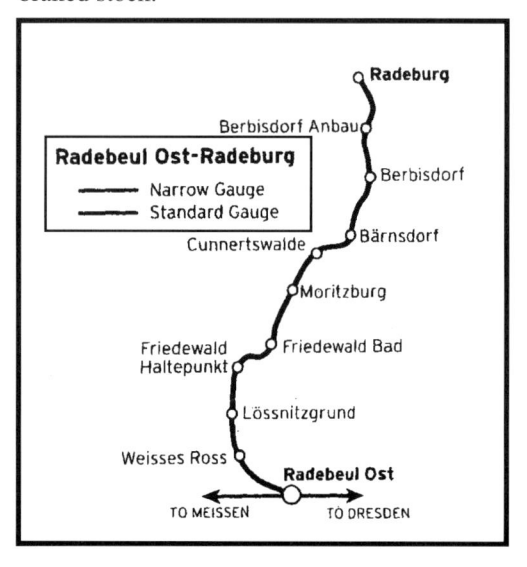

4.1. Two LKM 2-10-2Ts, nos 099 743-7 (99 779) and 099 742-9 (99 778) were seen on shed at Radebeul Öst in the suburbs of Dresden in June 1995. Both locomotives were being prepared for duty on the 16.55km line to Radeburg. (J.Marsh).

4.2. Restored to its original Saxon State Railway green livery and number, 0-4-4-0T Meyer no.132 (99 539) was resting outside Radebeul shed after working a tradzüg to Radeburg on 3rd May 1992. Note that the Heberlein brake equipment has been retained, although not in use. (B.Benn)

4.3. 2-10-2T no.099 743-7 (originally 99 779) storms across the tracks of the Dresden tram system at Weisses Ross with a passenger train bound for Radeburg in June 1995. (J.Marsh).

4.4. Another view of the level crossing at Weisses Ross as no. 099 742-9 (99 778) leaves the station with a train bound for Radebeul on 23rd September 1995. (D.Trevor Rowe).

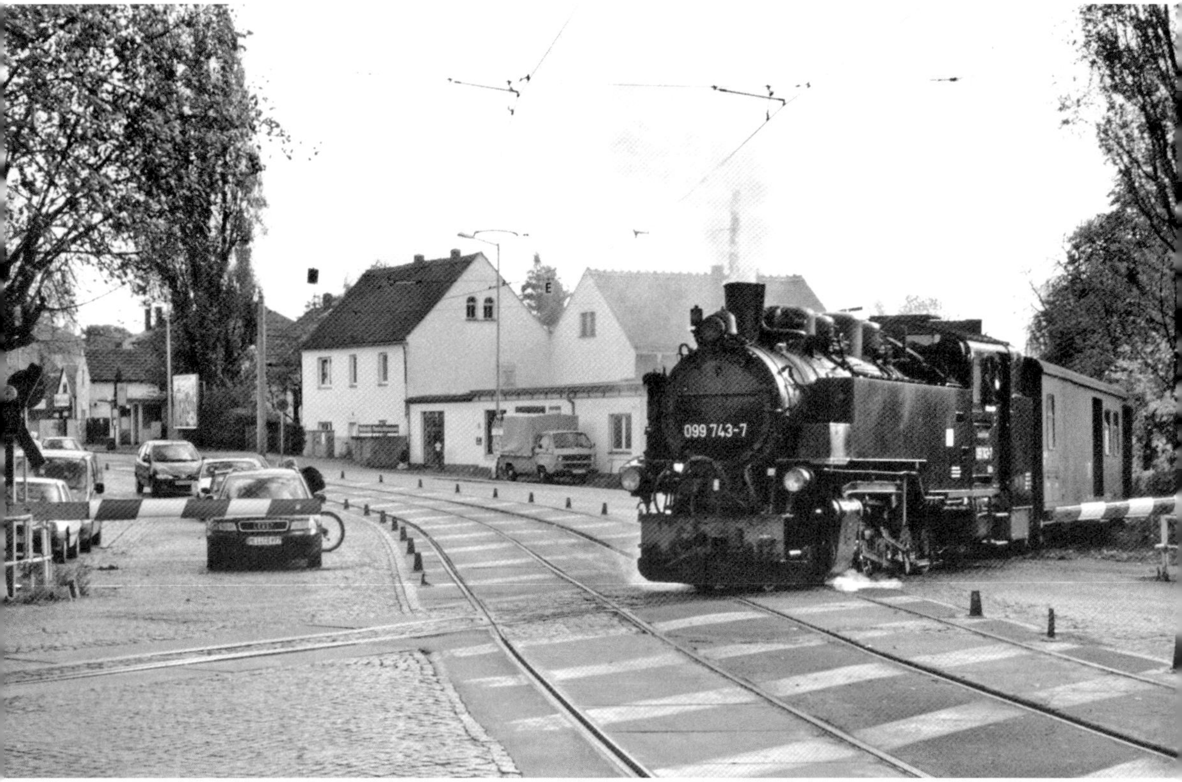
099 743-7

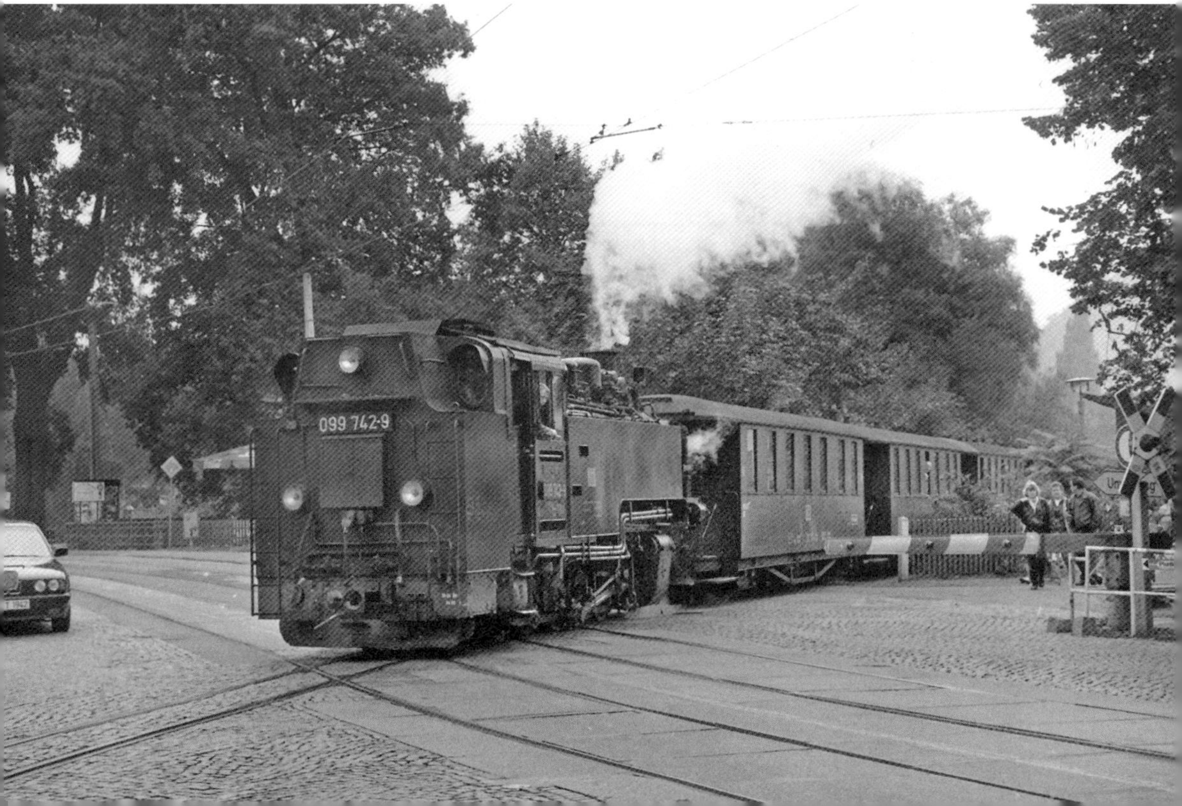
099 742-9

4.5. After leaving the suburbs of Dresden, the next station of importance is situated at Friedewald Bad. One of the later Class V11K neu 2-10-2Ts built by LKM in 1956, no. 099 742-9 was photographed departing with a Radebeul bound train on 23rd September 1995. (D.Trevor Rowe).

4.6. The major intermediate station on the Radebeul line is at Mortizburg. One of the last surviving Class V1K 0-10-0Ts, no. 99 713, was waiting in the loop whilst 2-10-2T no. 099 742-9 (99 778) is ready to depart with a train for Radeburg on 16th September 1995. (B.Benn).

4.7. Fresh from Meiningen works, immaculate Class V11K alt no. 99 1761-8 was about to depart from Mortizburg for Radebeul on 16th May 2004. The authors wife, Brenda Organ, admires the impressive locomotive whilst the crew exchange cheerful banter. (J.F.Organ).

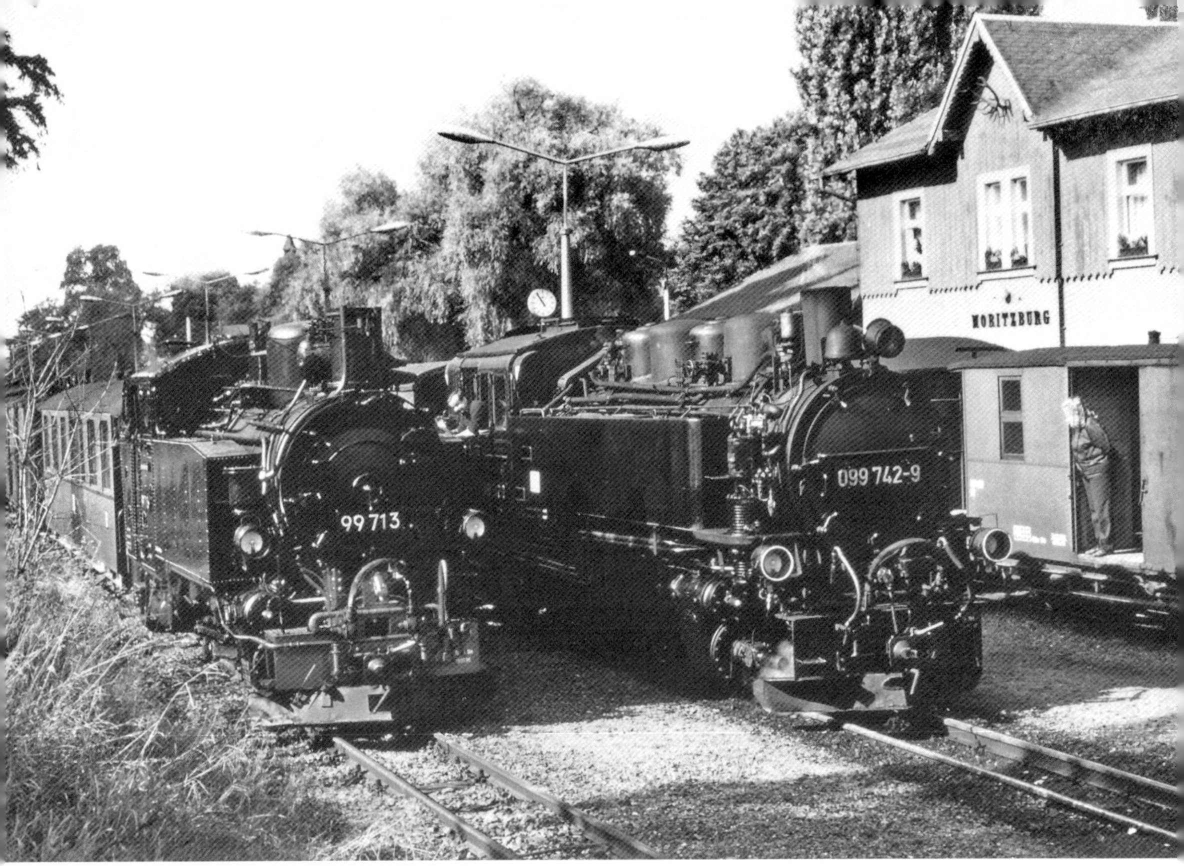
MORITZBURG
99 713
099 742-9

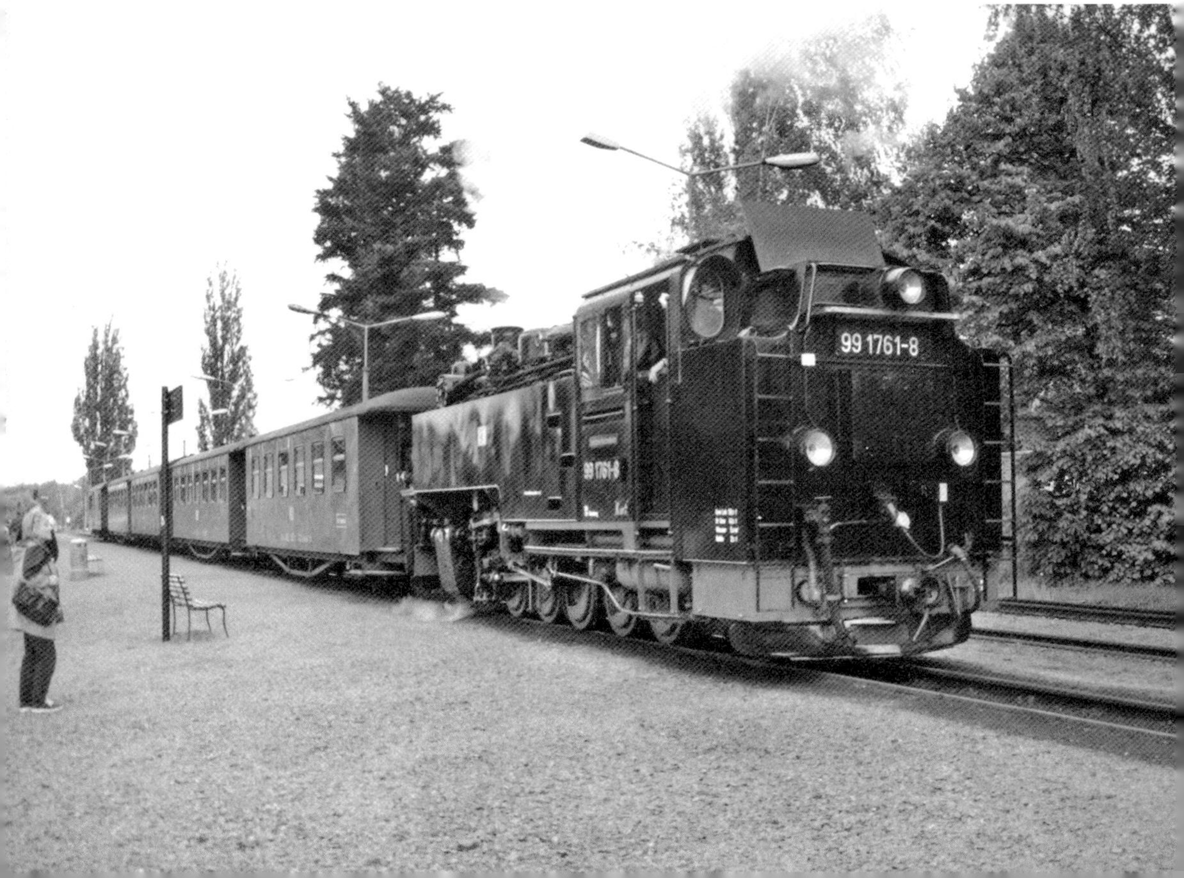
99 1761-8

4.8. Class V11K neu 2-10-2T no. 99 1777-4 was ready to depart from Radeburg with a train bound for Radebeul on 16th May 2004. This photograph was recorded during the final month of DB operation of the line, the last narrow gauge line to survive under their control. (J.F.Organ).

4.9. With no turntables on the line, bunker first running is the normal practice on the return journey to Radebeul. 2-10-2T no. 99 1779-0 departs from Radeburg on a bright Autumn day in October 2002. (J.Marsh).

4.10. Prior to the return journey, the locomotives replenish their water supply and the motion receives the attention of an oilcan. No. 99 1777-4 stands outside the shed at Radeburg whilst the driver issues instructions to his colleague on the footplate. This timeless scene was recorded on 16th May 2004, the authors 63rd birthday! (J.F.Organ).

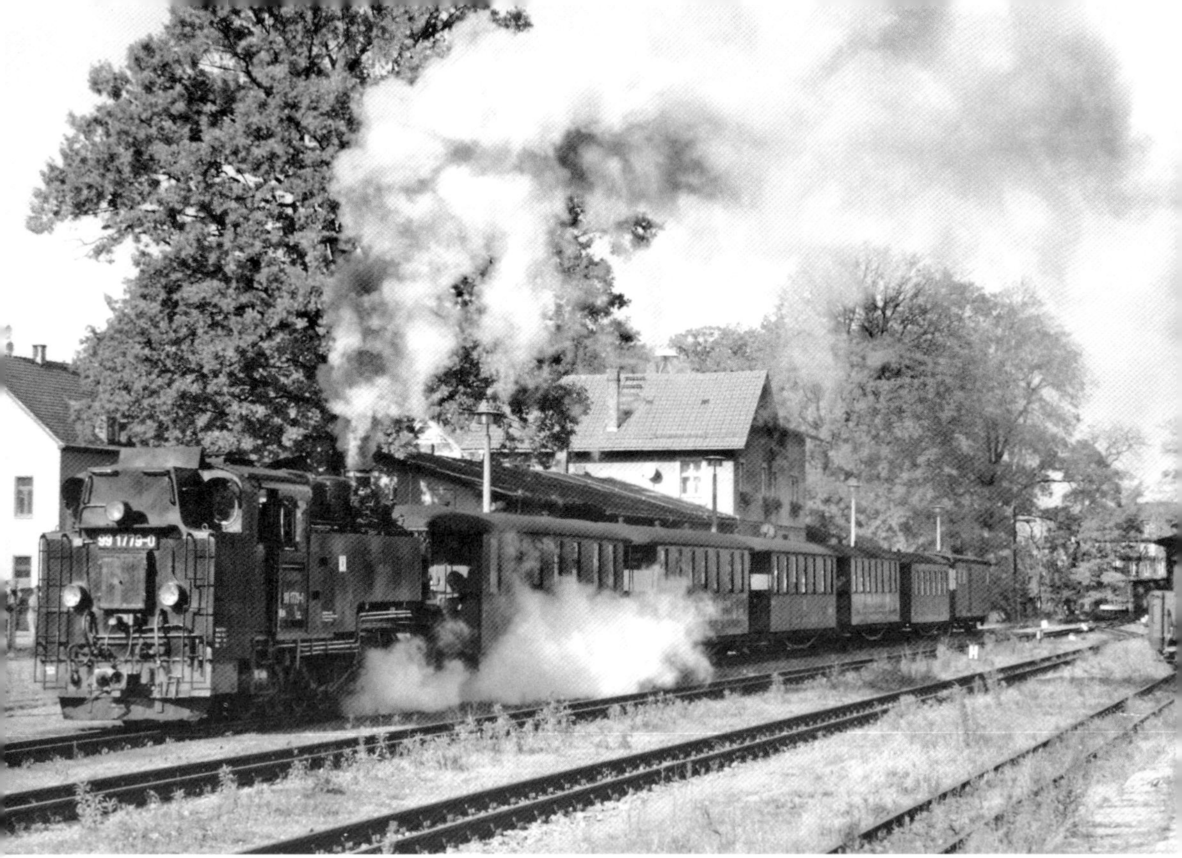
99 1779-0

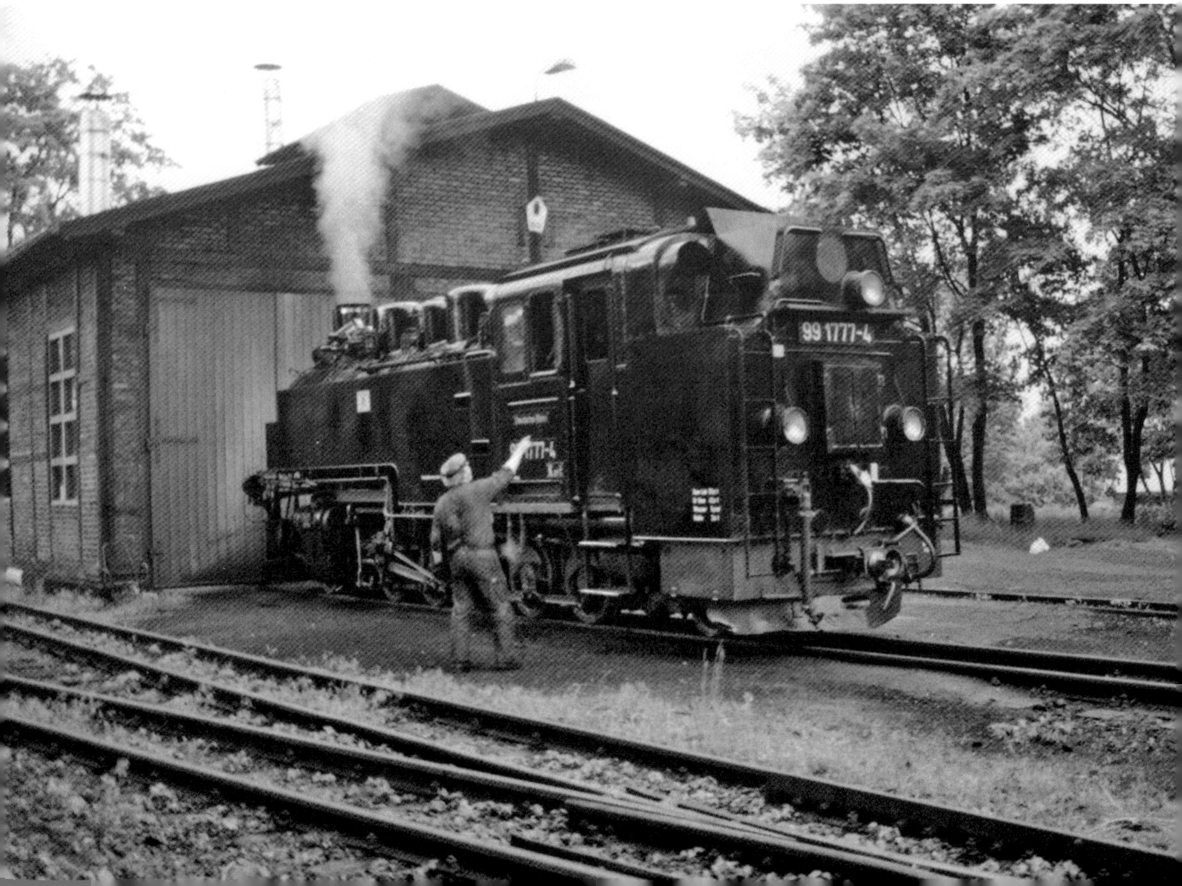
99 1777-4

5. Oschatz –Mügeln -Kemmlitz

This 17km line is the last remaining section of the complex 73km system of lines radiating from Mügeln, which in turn connected with the Wilsdruff network. Apart from this surviving section, the remainder of the system closed between 1964 and 1972. The survival of this predominately freight carrying line was due to the large kaolin works at Kemmlitz. The 75cm line was retained in order to transport the kaolin to the main line interchange at Oschatz.

Opened between Oschatz and Mügeln in 1885, with an extension to Kemmlitz and Kroptewitz in 1903, the line has always been associated with its fleet of Saxon-Meyers which were the only motive power employed on the route since their introduction in 1892. It was one of the first narrow gauge lines to transport freight in standard gauge vehicles carried on rollwagen transporters. Passenger traffic had mainly been "workers trains" in connection with the kaolin works, although a certain amount of public transport services were also catered for.

The steam hauled freight services continued until 1993 when, following the formation of Deutsche Bahn the line was privatised and diesel locomotives acquired to assist the venerable Meyers. Realising the tourist potential to be gained from operating steam hauled passenger trains, the new owners Pro Bahn marketed the line as the Döllnitzbahn and began weekend tourist services from 1994. Three Meyers remained at Mügeln, nos 99 1561, 99 1574 and 99 1584, to haul these trains. In addition to the tourist operation they have also been used to assist the diesel locomotives during the week on freight duties. This interesting operation is a true survivor from the multitude of mainly industrial lines that operated in the area, although the tourist service is facing an uphill struggle to survive and was only operating on a monthly basis in 2004.

The line leaves the outskirts of Oschatz crossing a low curved bridge over the River Döllnitz, the course of which is then followed for much of the 11.40km to Mügeln. After passing through a rural area of meadows and farms, Mügeln is approached between the rear of the houses and factories of the town. The depot and many sidings are situated here, Mügeln having been an important junction in the original network of lines. The final 5.60km to Kemmlitz is more industrialised, which somehow adds to the character of this fascinating operation which combines the tourist market of the present day with the industrial traffic for which the line was originally conceived.

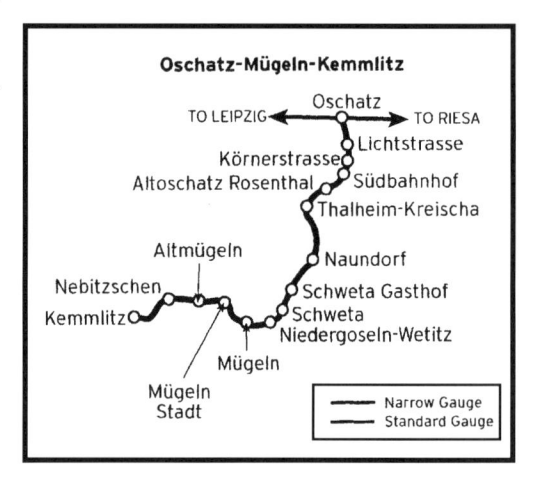

5.1. 0-4-4-0T Saxon-Meyer no. 99 1574-5 was recorded arriving at Oschatz with a passenger train from Kemmlitz. The Dollnitzbahn began operating occasional weekend tourist trains in 1995, such as this one recorded in June of that year. (J.Marsh).

5.2. The somewhat untidy surroundings of Oschatz station form the background to this view of no. 99 1574-5 running around its train, prior to returning to Kemmlitz on the same occasion. (J.Marsh).

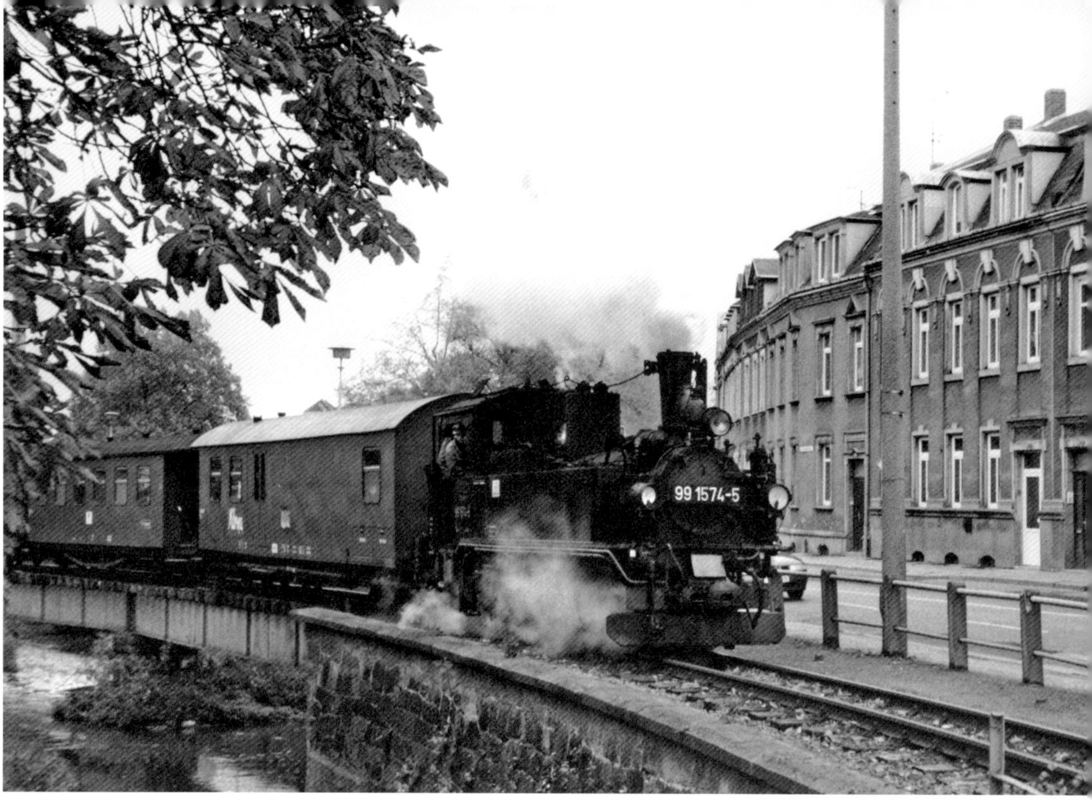
99 1574-5

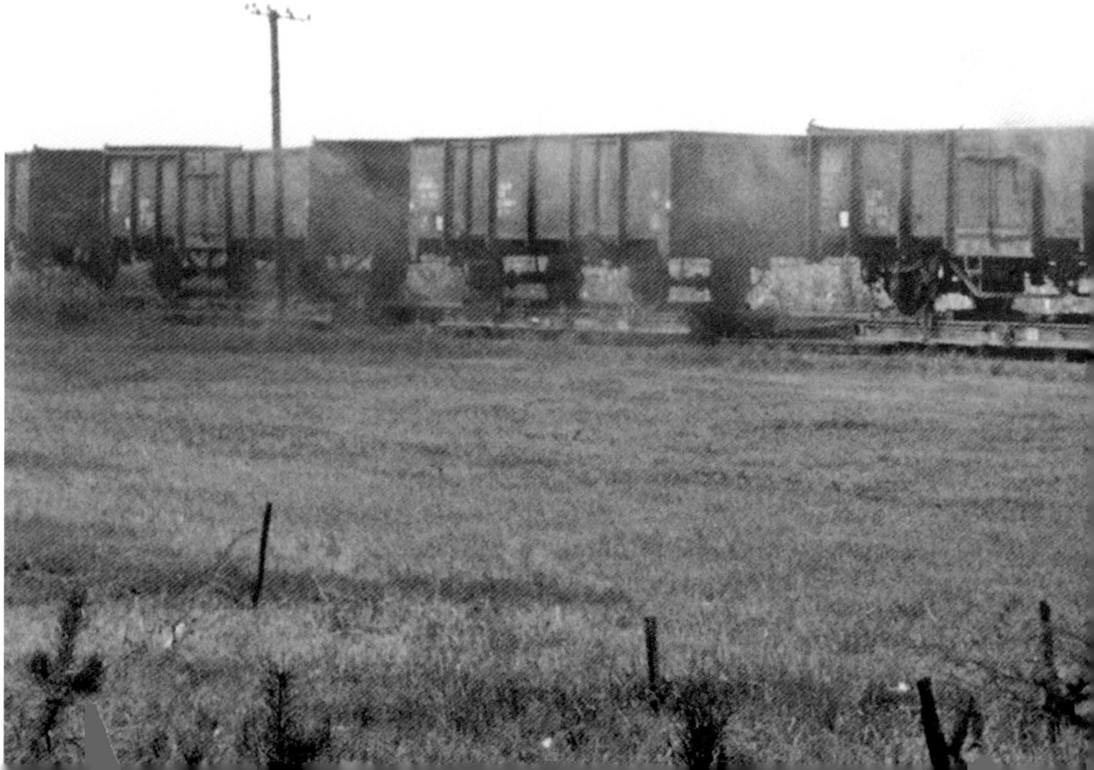

5.3. No. 99 1574-5 crossed the River Dollnitz as it departed from Oschatz at the commencement of its return journey to Mügeln and Kemmlitz in June 1995. (J.Marsh).

5.4. A more characteristic view of the Kemmlitz operation in its role as a freight carrying line shows a Saxon-Meyer hauling a heavy load of kaolin in standard gauge wagons between Mügeln and Oschatz on 29th August 1990. (J.Wiseman).

5.5. With the standard gauge van towering above the diminutive Meyer, no.99 1582-8 hauled a freight train across the flat landscape between Oschatz and Mügeln on the same occasion. (J.Wiseman).

5.6. No. 99 1582-8 negotiated an ungated level crossing at Mügeln whilst returning empty wagons to the kaolin works at Kemmlitz on 29th August 1990. Note that the person in charge of the crossing had no flags or high visibility clothing to warn road traffic of the train movement! (J.Wiseman).

5.7. Having completed its daily duties, Meyer no.99 1574-5 was viewed inside the locomotive shed at Mügeln, during the final stages of disposal, in June 1995. (J.Marsh).

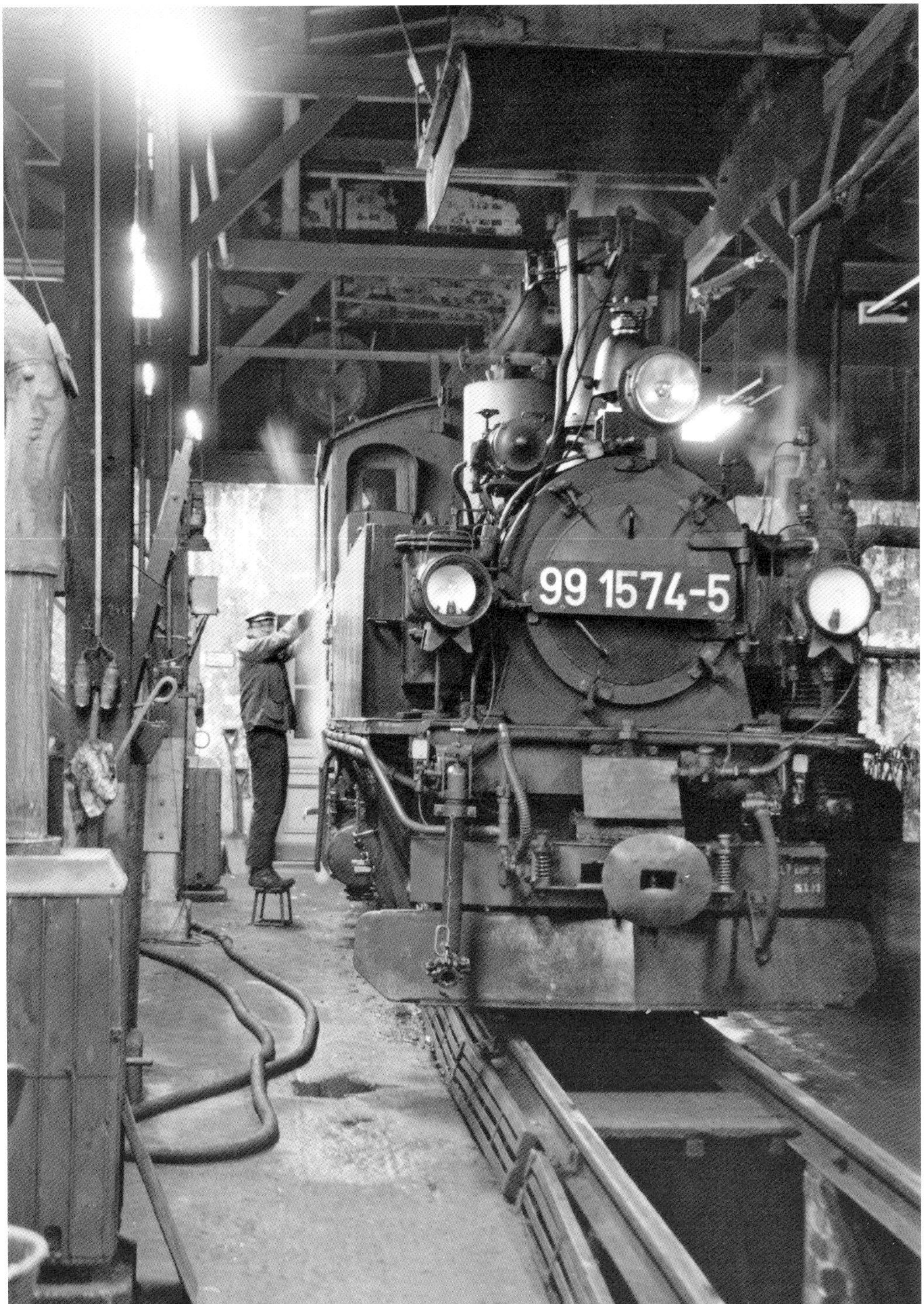
99 1574-5

5.8. Outside the same shed, sister locomotive no.099 708-0 (99 1582-8) was raising steam prior to a day's work hauling freight trains between Oschatz and Kemmlitz on 6th April 1992. (B.Benn).

5.9. Meyer no. 099 707-2, since renumbered 99 1574-5, was shunting standard gauge freight vans in the extensive narrow gauge yard at Kemmlitz on 6th April 1992. Part of the works conveyor belt loading system can be seen alongside the locomotive. (B.Benn).

6. Zittau-Kurort Oybin and Kurort Jonsdorf

Situated in the southeast corner of Saxony, close to the borders of Poland and the Czech Republic, this 14.40km "Y" shaped line linking Zittau with the Kurort Oybin and Kurort Jonsdorf was literally saved from closure by reunification. Originally a privately owned concern, it was absorbed by the Saxon State Railways in 1906. Opened in 1890, it was an extension of a 13.72km line linking Zittau and Markersdorf which had begun operations in 1884. In 1900 Markersdorf was linked to Hermsdorf via a 2.20km extension. The eastern section between Zittau and Hermsdorf was closed in 1945, leaving the two western arms to provide a connection with the main line network at Zittau. In addition to the passenger traffic serving the two health resorts at Oybin and Jonsdorf, the main reason for the continued survival of the line was a large open cast lignite mine near Zittau which produced large quantities of the poor quality brown coal commonly found in Eastern Europe.

Shortly before the reunification of Germany, plans to extend the mining operations at Zittau were announced. Had these plans gone ahead, the narrow gauge railway would have been severed and closed, road transport replacing rail shipment. With the collapse of the Iron Curtain, supplies of far superior coal became available from the West resulting in the demise of the Zittau mining operation. As a result the railway survived, principally as a passenger carrying operation. In a final act of defiance, the eight V11K alt 2-10-2T locomotives were converted to oil firing at Görlitz shortly after DB assumed responsibility for the operation of the line, this being a "guinea pig" for conversions elsewhere. In fact, no other 75cm lines under DB control were converted before they were transferred to the private sector. Following privatisation, the locomotives based at Zittau were converted back to coal firing, although using far better quality fuel than that available during the GDR era. In addition to the working fleet of 2-10-2Ts, an Orenstein & Koppel 0-8-0T no. 99 4532-0 is based at Bertsdorf. This locomotive was originally in service on the Trusetalbahn in Thüringen and transferred to the Zittau line in 1962.

During 1998, operation of the Zittau system was transferred to Sächsisch-Oberlausitzer Eisenbahngesellschaft (SOEG) who have introduced a service aimed primarily at the tourist market.

With both Kurorts offering differing attractions there is sufficient traffic on both branches to provide a viable operation. Kurort Oybin is noted for its medieval castle and monastery whilst Kurort Jonsdorf is famed for its mills and weaving industry. In addition both are situated in the foothills of the mountains and provide a suitable base for climbers and hikers, with a choice of stations from which to start and finish their expeditions.

The first 9km from Zittau Hauptbahnhof to the principal intermediate station and junction at Bertsdorf runs mainly through the suburbs of Zittau, passing many closed factories and the remnants of the once thriving mining activity. One aspect of reunification has been the decline of local industry in favour of large scale manufacturing in the industrial centres of the West. Leaving the terminus at Zittau, which is situated alongside the main line station, the 75cm rails descend steeply before passing under the standard gauge viaduct that spans part of the town. The line then passes through the suburbs until Zittau Süd is reached, after which the ascent to the hills begins in earnest. Once clear of the suburban sprawl, the route enters an area of pastoral charm before reaching the delightful station at Bertsdorf, with its small overall roof spanning the principal platform. Based in the locomotive shed at Bertsdorf is a supporting society that maintains the aforementioned 0-8-0T no. 99 4532-0 and a Saxon-Meyer no. 99 555 that until recently had stood on a plinth at Gera in Thüringen.

Upon leaving Bertsdorf, the two branches diverge almost immediately, with some trains timed to leave simultaneously. The best viewpoint to witness this performance is from the signal box conveniently situated between the two lines. The two 5km branches are quite different on the routes to their

Zittau - Kurort Oybin/Kurort Jonsdorf

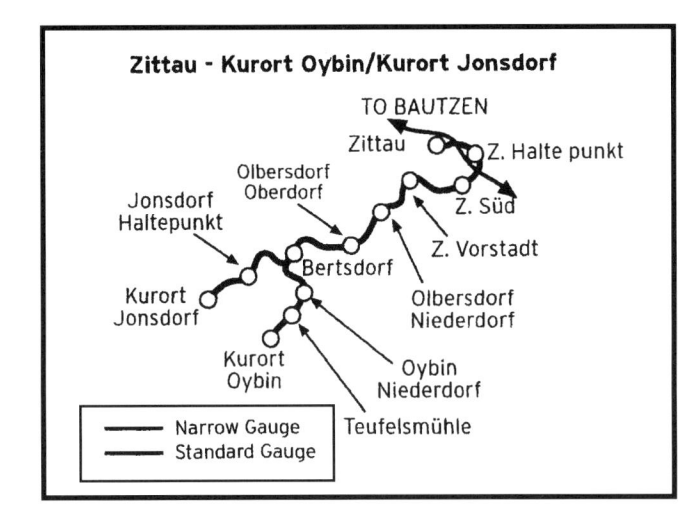

respective termini amid an area of splendid scenery, far removed from that encountered at the beginning of the journey from Zittau. The Jonsdorf line climbs steeply through woodland before emerging above the village whilst the route to Oybin is on a gentle grade through a very scenic valley to the terminus dominated by a huge cliff face. The whole operation is a veritable time warp being symbolic of the type of rural operation that used to be found throughout Europe as well as in Germany.

6.1. Class V11K alt 2-10-2T no. 99 1749-3 was recorded hauling standard gauge wagons near Zittau Hbf on 28th August 1990. This section of the route is a connecting line between the narrow gauge and standard gauge sidings. (J.Wiseman).

6.2. At the same location, 2-10-2T no. 99 758 is arriving at Zittau Hbf station from the depot prior to hauling a passenger train to Kurort Oybin on 15th May 2004. (J.F.Organ).

6.3. During a visit from its normal base at Mügeln, Meyer no.99 584 was captured departing from Zittau Süd with a special charter train to Kurort Jonsdorf in August 1996. (J.Marsh).

6.4. With an industrial backdrop, 2-10-2T no. 099 730-4 (99 757) is climbing away from Zittau Süd with a passenger train bound for Bertsdorf and one of the Kurorts on 6th April 1992. (B.Benn).

6.5.　A more detailed view of the same locomotive was taken as it continued its climb away from Zittau Süd during April 1992. At that time, the Zittau based locomotives were running as oil burners during a short experimental period. (B.Benn).

6.6.　Saxon-Meyer no. 99 584 posed alongside two Class V11K alt 2-10-2Ts, nos 99 787 and 99 735, at Bertsdorf in August 1996. No. 99 735 was about to depart for Kurort Oybin whilst the Meyer was preparing for the steep ascent to Kurort Jonsdorf. (J.Marsh).

6.7. The skyline of Zittau recedes into the background as 2-10-2T no.099 724-7 (99 735) departs from Zittau Vorstadt on 20th September 1995. The buildings just visible alongside the locomotive were part of the former coal mining concern that so nearly brought about a premature closure of the railway, had their plans for expansion gone ahead. (B.Benn).

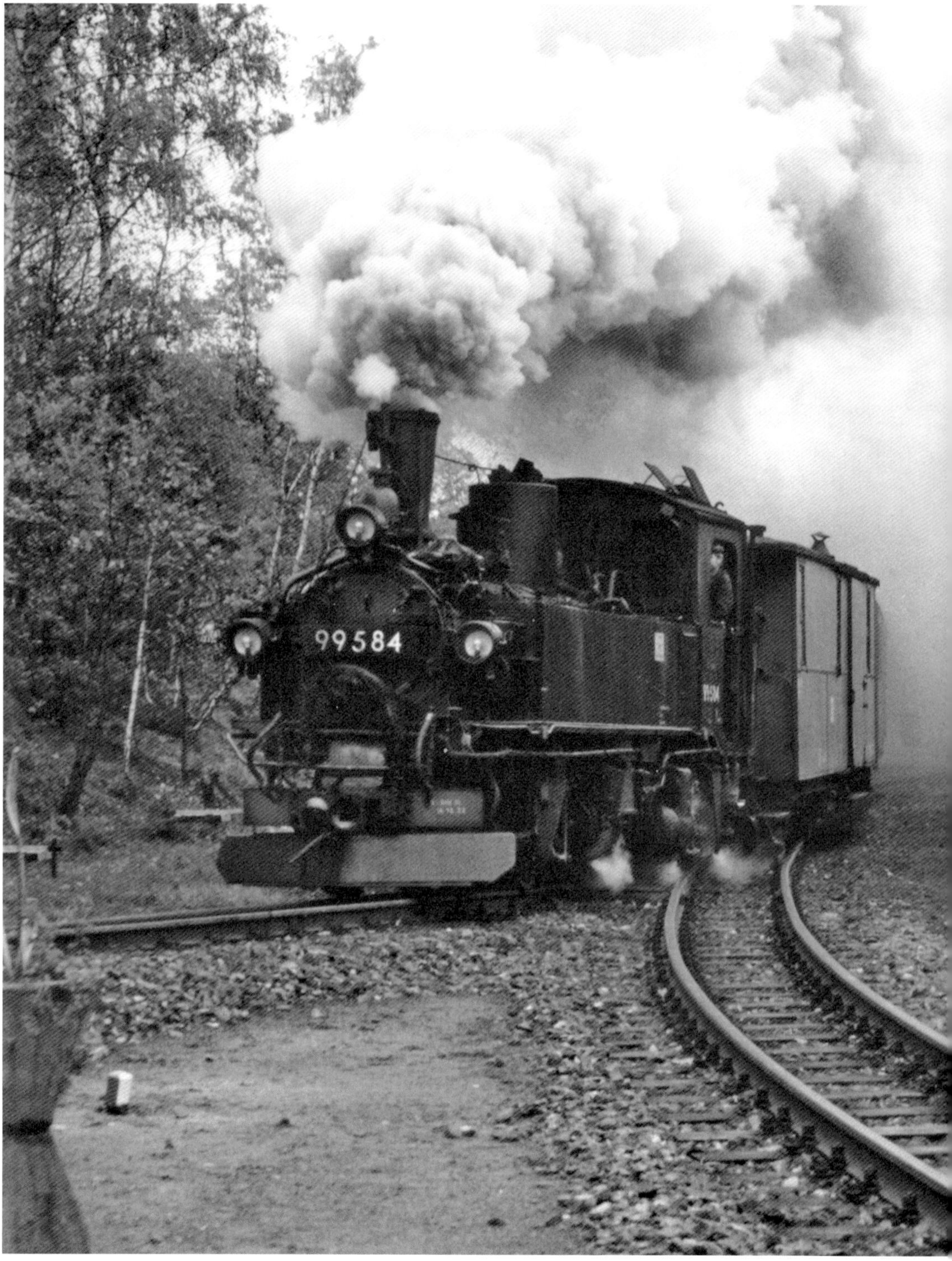
99584

6.8. Smoke and steam abound as the two locomotives diverged onto their respective branch lines almost immediately after leaving Bertsdorf station. The photographer was standing alongside the signal box, which is conveniently situated in the "Y" between the two lines. (J.Marsh).

6.9. A rather more sedate departure from Bertsdorf was made by 2-10-2T no. 099 731-2 (99 758) as it began the ascent to Kurort Jonsdorf on 9th August 1993. Bertsdorf is the only remaining junction on the surviving 75cm lines in Saxony. (B.Benn).

6.10. At the summit of the climb from Bertsdorf, 2-10-2T no. 99 749 negotiates the level crossing before entering the outskirts of Kurort Jonsdorf at the intermediate station, Jonsdorf Haltestelle, on 15th May 2004. (J.F.Organ).

6.11. No. 99 758 runs into the headshunt at Kurort Jonsdorf prior to running around the train it had just hauled from Zittau. The alpine nature of the scenery and architecture can be seen in this view recorded on 15th May 2004. (J.F.Organ).

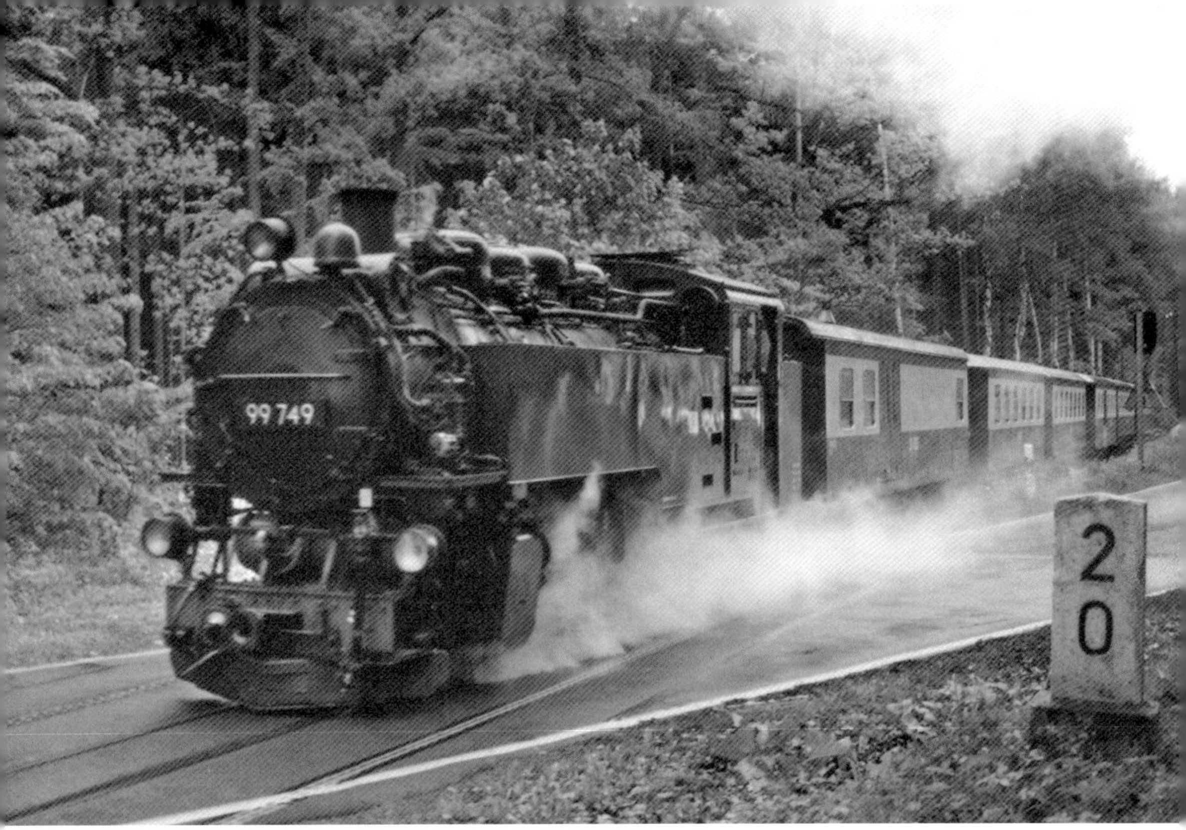
99 749
20

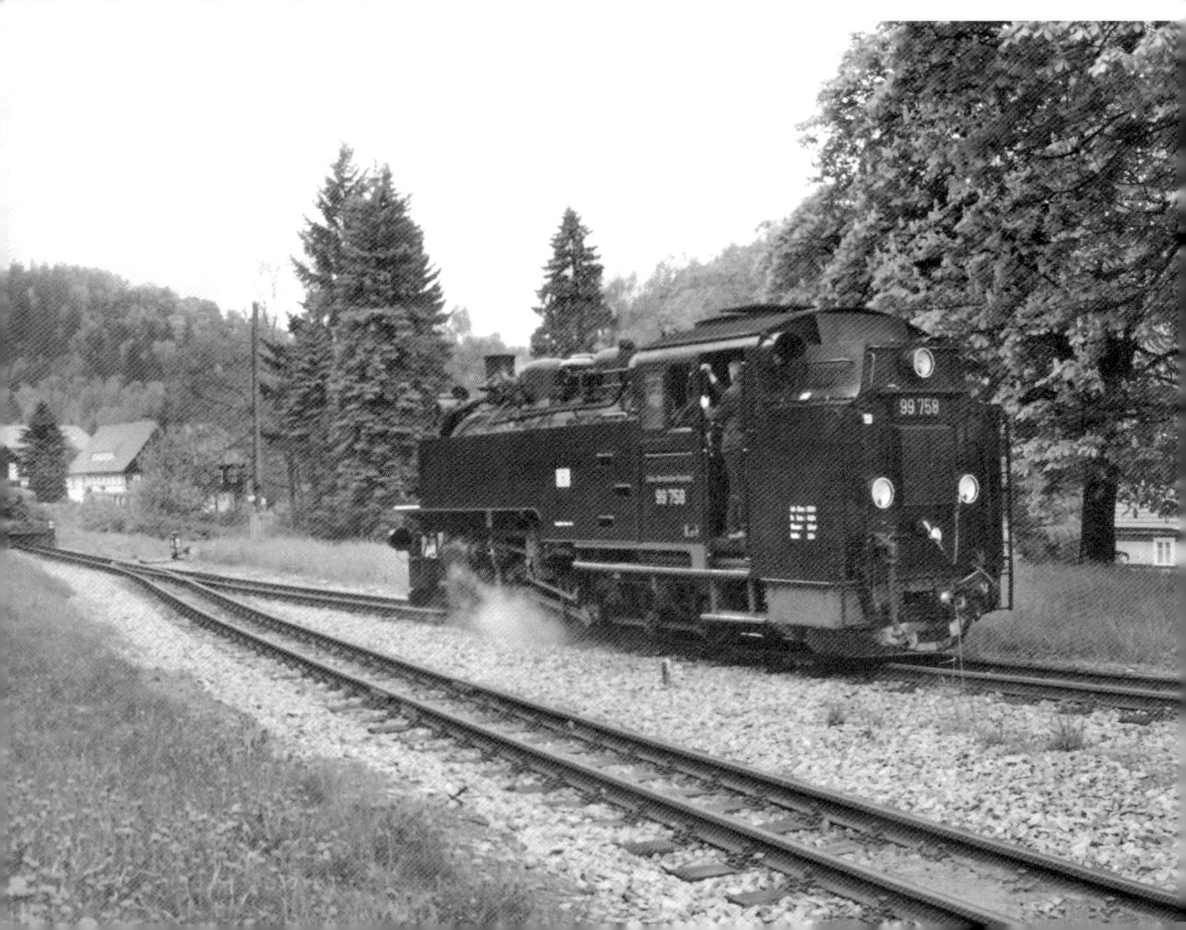
99 758
99 758

6.12. On the easier graded branch to Kurort Oybin, 2-10-2T no. 99 1757-6 was viewed departing from Bertsdorf, during the course of its journey to the terminus on 28th August 1990. (J.Wiseman).

6.13. No. 99 1757-6 was recorded drifting through Teufelsmühle, about mid way between Bertsdorf and Kurort Oybin, on the same occasion. (J.Wiseman).

7. Cranzahl to Kurort Oberwiesenthal

This scenic 17.35km line is situated in the south of Saxony, close to the Czech border. Opened in 1897, it has always been principally a passenger carrying line to serve the resort of Kurort Oberwiesenthal situated high in the Erzgebirge. Freight traffic has largely been of a domestic nature, there being no centres of industry along the route. An all year round service has been provided, the upper terminus being a popular venue for winter sports activities. Contrary to popular belief, even during the days of oppression under communist rule, the citizens of East Germany were allowed the freedom to enjoy themselves! With a number of hotels and other concerns at Kurort Oberwiesenthal involved with the activities of the resort, many of which relied on staff who commuted from Cranzahl, the early morning and late evening services were a well known feature of this interesting route.

As with the other narrow gauge lines that survived reunification, DB were anxious to dispose of this operation despite the fact that it was heavily patronised throughout the year. In June 1998, the line was taken over by BVO Bahn GmbH, a local bus company with its headquarters at Oberwiesenthal. Their first act was to rename their newly acquired railway the Fichtelbergbahn, whilst on a less positive note the number of services were reduced, the revised timetable being aimed at the tourist market rather than the commuter traffic. Consequently the historic early and late departures were abandoned, being replaced by buses. However, the new owners have invested heavily with improvements to the infrastructure and equipment. The old locomotive shed at Oberwiesenthal was demolished during 2003 and replaced with an impressive new combined depot and workshop. Although a new building, it has been built to a traditional design that blends into the surroundings in complete accord.

Since their introduction during the 1950s, the locomotives most closely associated with this line have been the class V11K neu 2-10-2Ts, of which six examples have been based at Cranzahl or Oberwiesenthal during the last decade. Prior to the introduction of these relatively modern machines, Saxon-Meyers or the earlier version of 2-10-2Ts had been used on the line.

Cranzahl is situated on a standard gauge branch line that runs south from Chemnitz to the Czech border at Vejprty. A cross platform interchange with the narrow gauge route allows an easy transfer, as with most of the dual gauge stations in Saxony. Leaving Cranzahl the narrow gauge line passes through a largely agricultural area until the first major station and principal passing point at Neudorf is reached. Leaving Neudorf there is a short section of roadside running after which the line enters an area of woodland, passing another intermediate station at Vierenstrasse en route. Emerging from the forest is another passing loop at Kretscham, after which the line begins to climb into the mountains. The major intermediate station is at Hammerunterwiesenthal where another passing loop is situated along with sidings and a goods shed.

Leaving Hammerunterwiesenthal, the steepest part of the route is encountered as it runs alongside a small stream that marks the border with the Czech Republic. The approach to Kurort Oberwiesenthal is across a slender trestle viaduct, 110 metres in length and 23 metres high, which is a favourite location for photographers and observers at this mountain resort. At an altitude of 893m, the station at the upper terminus is the highest in Saxony, second only to the Brocken on the Harz system. Oberwiesenthal also holds the distinction of being the highest town in Germany.

The Fichtelbergbahn remains one of the most attractive steam operated narrow gauge lines in Germany. Combining steep gradients and splendid mountain scenery, this line has a secure future thanks to its enthusiastic new owners. Fortunately there is sufficient tourist traffic in the area to justify its continued survival.

For much of its route the railway is parallel to a scenic footpath, which is the southern section of a long distance path. This runs from Rügen on the Baltic coast to Oberwiesenthal on the Czech border, a distance of approximately 700km.

Cranzahl - Oberwiesenthal

TO ANNABERG - BUCHHOLZ

Cranzahl
Unterneudorf
Neudorf
Vierenstrasse
Kretscham - Rothensehma
Niederschlag
Hammerunterwiesenthal
Unterwiesenthal
Kurort Oberwiesenthal

—— Narrow Gauge
—— Standard Gauge

7.1. The 75cm gauge line to Kurort Oberwiesenthal connects with the scenic standard gauge route from Chemnitz to the Czech border at Vejprty. During 2003 this line was closed whilst track renewal and other repairs to the infrastructure were carried out. The line was reopened in early 2004, operated with sleek modern two-car diesel units, one of which was recorded arriving at Cranzahl on 19th May 2004. Services are timed to coincide on both lines, thereby continuing the pattern established when both were operated by Deutsche Reichsbahn. (Mrs.B.Organ).

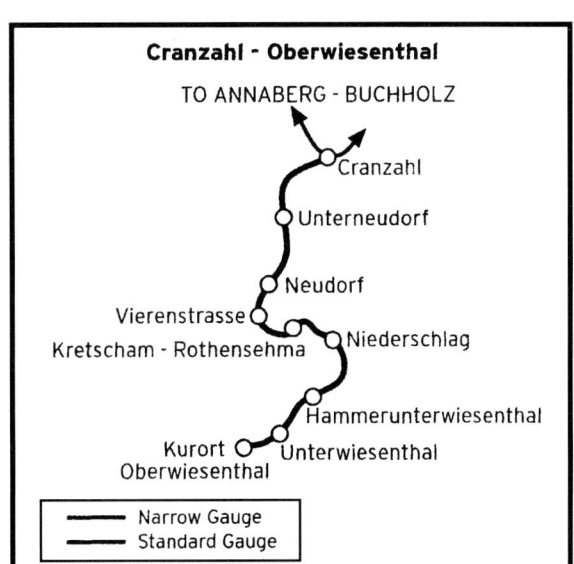

7.2. Having exchanged passengers, 2-10-2T no.99 794 departs from Cranzahl with the early afternoon departure for Oberwiesenthal on the same occasion. The locomotive faced an almost unbroken climb of up to 1 in 30 during the 17km journey, the only respite being through the stations where the gradient is less severe. (J.F.Organ).

7.3. Around the time of reunification, 2-10-2T no. 99 1734-5 approaches Neudorf with a train from Cranzahl to Oberwiesenthal on 26th August 1990. At that period, Class V11Ks of both types were still working on the line, the earlier versions having been transferred elsewhere before the line was privatised in 1998. (J.Wiseman).

7.4. Neudorf is the principal passing place on the route. Class V11K neu no.99 785 was arriving with an Oberwiesenthal bound train, whilst sister locomotive no.99 794 was waiting in the loop with a down train on 19th May 2004. (J.F.Organ).

7.5. Class V11K alt no.99 1734-5 arrives at Neudorf with a train from Kurort Oberwiesenthal. This section of the line includes a short attractive stretch of roadside running, as seen in this view recorded on 26th August 1990. (J.Wiseman).

7.6. Class V11K neu no.99 1781-6 is passing over a slender bridge between Vierenstrasse and Neudorf, with a Cranzahl bound train on the same date. (J.Wiseman).

7.7. LKM 2-10-2T no.99 789 was seen accelerating away from Hammerunterwiesenthal with an early morning train bound for the upper terminus in August 1967. (T.Martin).

7.8. A winter scene in the Ergebirge includes 2-10-2T no. 099 750-2 (99 786) crossing the viaduct on the approach to Kurort Oberwiesenthal on 14th March 1996. Due to its easy access, this is one of the most popular viewpoints on the Fichtelbergbahn. (B.Benn).

7.9. In less hostile conditions, 2-10-2T no.99 785 was viewed crossing the viaduct with a train from Cranzahl during the late afternoon of 18th May 2004. (J.F.Organ).

7.10. LKM 2-10-2T no.99 789 was photographed having its coal bunker refilled outside the old locomotive shed at Kurort Oberwiesenthal in August 1967. (T.Martin).

7.11. Nine years later, 2-10-2T no.99 1790-7 replenished its water tank at the same location on 21st April 1976. As Kurort Oberwiesenthal is the highest town in Germany, the locomotive depot must also be at the highest altitude of any building of its type. (K.Taylorson).

7.12. The recently constructed replacement depot and workshop complex forms an impressive backdrop to this view of an immaculate Class V11K neu 2-10-2T no.99 794 on 18th May 2004. The locomotive had just re-entered service following a major overhaul. (J.F.Organ).

8. Preservation in Saxony

The Erzgebirge area of Saxony is the location of no less than three preservation schemes devoted to the Saxon narrow gauge railways in addition to the Fichtelbergbahn. These are all situated a short distance from Kurort Oberwiesenthal, which makes this area an even more attractive destination for anyone intent upon exploring these remaining survivors from the once extensive network of lines.

Oberrittersgrün Museum

When the 9.36km line between Grünstädtel and Oberrittersgrün closed in September 1971, the southern terminus was officially designated as a museum site. Since 1972 a large collection of historic rolling stock and artefacts has been collected and restored to a high standard. The complex includes the station building, loco shed and goods yard, all of which have been retained in their original condition as a lasting reminder of these rural stations in their heyday. Some of the passenger coaches have had their interiors adapted to incorporate display panels portraying the history of the Sächsen 75cm systems. The displays include detailed photographs of all the various types of locomotive that have worked on the Saxon lines since 1881.

The pride of the collection is to be found in the loco shed where Saxon-Meyer no.99 579, which hauled the last train from Grünstädtel, has been beautifully restored as a static exhibit. In addition to the Meyer, a number of industrial locomotives from quarries in the area have been added to the collection. These include a 0-4-0WT built by Orenstein & Koppel in 1912 and a pair of former Heeresfeldbahn Gmeinder diesel locomotives. A type K57 Einheitslok class V11K alt 2-10-2T no. 99 1759-2 has recently joined the collection.

Museumbahn Schönheide

Opened between 1881 and 1897, the 41.85km line between Wilkau-Hasslau and Carlsfeld was the first and longest of the independent Saxon lines. Closed in stages between 1967 and 1979, the last section to remain in operation was near the southern end of the line at Schönheide, which was retained to serve local industry.

Since the complete closure of the line, the station complex at Schönheide Mitte has been acquired by a preservation group with the intention of reopening a short length of the route as a tourist operation. Initially, 2km between Schönheide and Neuheide was restored by 1995, this being increased to 5km in 2001 when the line was reopened to Stützengrün. Although the group would like to extend the operation at each end there are problems, such as a missing viaduct and building development over the track bed, which will thwart their future plans.

The collection includes three Saxon-Meyers, nos 99 516, 99 582 and 99 585. Of these the first two are in working order whilst the other is to be restored when time and money allows the work to be carried out. The few items of rolling stock have been restored to a high standard, being painted in the DR green livery. Being a wholly volunteer organisation, progress is naturally limited to the financial recourses available. However they are a very enthusiastic, albeit small, group who will no doubt succeed in restoring more of their acquisitions in the not too distant future. Due to the volunteer nature of the organisation, services only operate at weekends during the summer months.

Pressnitztalbahn

Situated a short distance to the east of Cranzahl was the 22.95km line linking Wolkenstein and Jöhstadt. This attractive route, which was particularly scenic at its southern end, succumbed to closure in 1986. However the scenic attributes of this section led to the formation of a dynamic preservation group known as the Pressnitztalbahn based at Jöhstadt.

By 1994 the new organisation had succeeded in reopening 2km of the route northwards to Schlössel with further extensions added during the latter half of the 1990s. By 2001 Steinbach, the major intermediate station on the old route, 8km from Jöhstadt and ultimate aim of the society, had been achieved. The stations and infrastructure have all been superbly restored to a high standard and is a credit to the dedication and expertise of this wholly volunteer group.

The Wolkenstein to Jöhstadt route was always a line associated with the splendid Saxon-Meyers and, not surprisingly, three examples of these historic locomotives have been preserved in working order on the Pressnitztalbahn. These are nos 99 1542, 99 1568 and 99 1590, all of which worked on the line in the pre-preservation era. Other locomotives in service at Jöhstadt include a 0-6-0T and two industrial diesels built by LKM in 1957. The 0-6-0T, no. 99 4511, has led a nomadic life working on numerous German 75cm lines. Built as a 0-6-2T by Krauss in 1899, it received a comprehensive rebuild at Görlitz in 1965 from where it emerged in its current condition. The diesel locomotives are used to haul passenger trains during the off peak periods, as well as being usefully employed for shunting duties. In addition a large collection of historic rolling stock of both passenger and freight vehicles has been restored, including rollwagen transporters complete with standard gauge wagons.

Located in a wooded valley, the steeply graded route between Steinbach and Jöhstadt provides a lasting reminder of the numerous Sächsen narrow gauge branch lines that were the lifeline of the rural communities of Saxony for so many years. The sight and sound of a Saxon-Meyer climbing the incline towards Jöhstadt, hauling a varied collection of historic stock is one that is not easily forgotten. The enthusiasm and vision of those responsible for saving this beautiful stretch of railway cannot be underestimated. One problem that the new organisation faced when they took over the site at Jöhstadt in 1990 was one of accessibility. A new block of austere flats had been built on the track bed between the station building and depot, which obviously rendered access to the original station impossible. However a compact station and depot complex has been successfully created in the limited space available. One result is a complex shunting arrangement after a train arrives from Steinbach. The locomotive pulls into a headshunt whilst another locomotive, normally a diesel, is attached to the rear of the train. When the passengers have disembarked, the diesel pulls the entire ensemble a short distance back down the line enabling the locomotive to enter the yard for watering and routine maintenance. The diesel engine then propels the rolling stock back into the platform road prior to the steam locomotive running back from the yard and coupling onto the train for the return journey.

As with the Museumbahn Schönheide, services are normally restricted to weekends and public holidays between May and October, although they also operate throughout the remainder of the year on specified dates. The immaculate state in which this delightful railway is presented is a credit to all those who have worked so hard to rebuild the line and its equipment during the last decade.

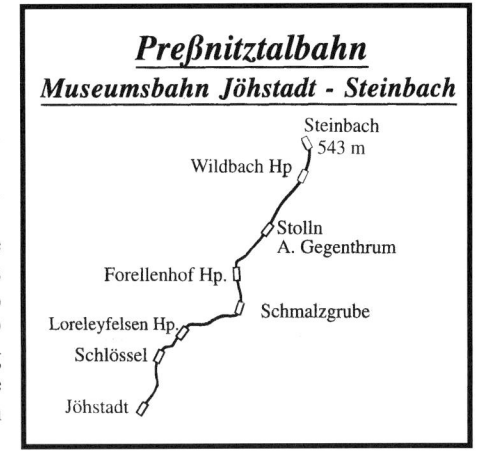

8.1. A scene at Oberrittersgrün in 1971, shortly before the line from Grünstadtel closed. A lorry of obvious Eastern European ancestry was loading timber onto a goods wagon whilst 0-4-4-0T Saxon-Meyer no.99 1568-7 was waiting to begin its journey. Following closure, the station and depot at Oberrittersgrün became the home of the official museum devoted to the Saxon narrow gauge systems. (K.Taylorson coll).

8.2. Early morning at Jöhstadt and three Saxon-Meyers are being prepared for service on the Pressnitztalbahn. No. 99 1568-7 takes water, 99 1590-1 raises steam whilst no. 99 1542-2 was about to leave with the first train to Schmalzgrube. Such intense activity is unusual even on this energetically operated museum line. This scene was recorded on the occasion of an enthusiast weekend on 11th February 1995, before the line was reopened to Steinbach. (B.Benn).

8.3. Meyer no. 99 1542-2 being shunted into the locomotive shed at Jöhstadt by one of the LKM diesel shunters in readiness for operation the following day. Note the Heberlein brake cable running from the cab to the front buffer beam, via a pulley attached to the chimney. Although many of the preserved Meyers have retained this primitive braking system, it is a purely decorative feature, vacuum braking being used in service. This scene was recorded on 19th May 2004. (J.F.Organ).

8.4. The same locomotive was viewed at Jöhstadt the following day, complete with floral decoration. 20th May 2004 was the annual Himmelfaht to celebrate Ascension Day, which is a public holiday in Germany. No.99 1542-2 was about to depart with a train for Steinbach on this most attractive railway. (Mrs.B.Organ).

8.5. The well travelled Krauss/Görlitz 0-6-0T no.99 4511-4 was at Jöhstadt, where it was recorded on static display on 20th May 2004. This locomotive was housed at Altenkirchen on Rügen in 1966, as recorded in North East German Narrow Gauge. (J.F.Organ).

8.6. Also decorated for the Himmelfaht celebrations was Meyer no. 99 1590-1, which was captured arriving at Jöhstadt with a train from Steinbach on the same occasion. (J.F.Organ).

8.7. Having been released from its rake of coaches, no.99 1590-1 had moved into the depot to replenish its water supply before returning down the valley with another train. (J.F.Organ).

8.8. The two Saxon-Meyers pass at Schmalzgrube, which is now the principal passing point on this delightful railway. No.99 1590-1 was arriving from Jöhstadt whilst no.99 1542-2 was waiting with a train from Steinbach on 20th May 2004. (J.F.Organ).

8.9. The driver of no.99 1590-1 concentrates on the road ahead as he draws into the platform at Schmalzgrube on the same occasion. (Mrs.B.Organ).

8.10. Meyer no.99 1590-1 departs from the former goods yard at Steinbach with a photo-charter mixed train on 19th May 2004. These activities are a regular feature on the surviving narrow gauge lines in Saxony. (J.F.Organ).

8.11. With standard gauge wagons mounted on rollwagen transporters in the background, no.99 1590-1 was recorded departing from Steinbach with its mixed train, heading up the valley for its next rendezvous with the photographers who had chartered the special. (J.F.Organ).

PART TWO - FORESTRY AND PARK RAILWAYS.

In addition to the extensive network of 75cm lines, Saxony also boasted a large 60cm forestry system and was among the pioneers in providing miniature railways in the parks of the major cities.

Part of the forestry line has now been converted into a tourist operation whilst, following many years of closure, the miniature lines have in the post war period been rejuvenated into successful ventures operated mainly by schoolchildren.

9. Waldeisenbahn Muskau.

In 1895 the first section of what was ultimately to become an extensive system of 60cm forestry railway was opened at Bad Muskau, near the present day Polish border. Built as a private venture on the estate of the Count of Arnim, its purpose was to serve the sawmills, lignite mines, paper and brick works that were located within the estate. Timber haulage was the major source of revenue although the other industries contributed their fair share of traffic. Ultimately the Muskauer Waldbahnen, as it was originally known, exceeded 80km with a standard gauge connection at Weisswasser to the main lines linking Cottbus, Frankfurt (Oder) and Görlitz.

Motive power was originally provided by some industrial 0-4-0Ts, which were supplied by Jung and Orenstein & Koppel, being adequate for the initial requirements. In addition to these smaller locomotives, Krauss of Munich supplied a 0-6-0TT in 1895 for hauling heavier loads on the main line of the system. After World War One an upsurge in traffic resulted in six of the ubiquitous Feldbahn 0-8-0Ts being acquired together with some larger industrial locomotives. The latter included a powerful Borsig 0-8-0T dating from 1912. Rolling stock comprised of a variety of open wagons suitable for haulage of the products connected with the various industries served by the system.

Following World War Two and the resultant boundary changes, most of the eastern section of the system was ceded to Poland whilst the remainder was within the newly formed GDR. In 1951 the German section was taken over by Deutsche Reichbahn and continued to operate under its new ownership in much the same way until economic factors forced its closure in 1978. Fortunately most of the equipment, including all of the locomotives, was preserved in either East or West Germany.

During 1992 a scheme to rebuild part of the system as a tourist operation was announced. By 1995 a total distance of 20km of track had been re-laid including the section linking Bad Muskau with the main line connection at Weisswasser. In addition the branch to Kromlau, which included a triangular junction near Weisswasser, was also reinstated. The route of the line, now renamed Waldeisenbahn Muskau, has been incorporated into an attractive country park that has been created to the south of Bad Muskau. Due to its main line connection, Weisswasser is the operating base for the line, with alternative trains running to Bad Muskau or Kromlau during a normal working day. Operations are confined mainly to weekends and public holidays between April and October, trains being hauled by both steam and diesel locomotives during the course of a day. The depot near Bad Muskau was rejuvenated to its former condition whilst some of the original locomotives and equipment were re-acquired, many having been preserved on plinths during the period of closure. These include the Borsig 0-8-0T, one of the Jung 0-4-0Ts and two of the Feldbahn 0-8-0Ts. In order to assist with the rebuilding of the line and to provide economical motive power during the quieter periods, some industrial diesel locomotives were also acquired.

During the last decade, the Waldeisenbahn Muskau has developed into a major tourist attraction. Much of the former forestry plantation has been landscaped into attractive parkland whilst its location, isolated from the other Saxon narrow gauge lines, provides a completely different customer base due to its close proximity to major centres such as Cottbus and Görlitz.

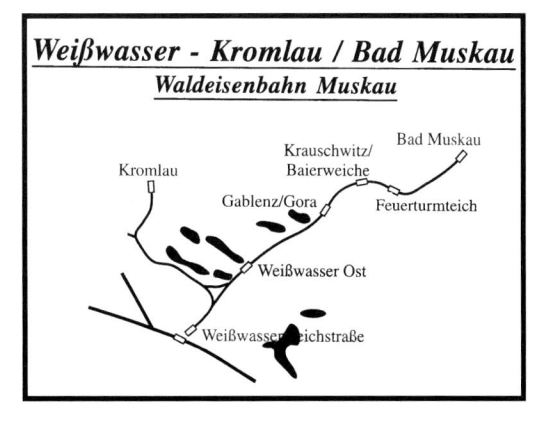

Weißwasser - Kromlau / Bad Muskau
Waldeisenbahn Muskau

Kromlau — Krauschwitz/Baierweiche — Bad Muskau
Gablenz/Gora — Feuerturmteich
Weißwasser Ost
Weißwasser Reichstraße

9.1.   Feldbahn 0-8-0T no. 99 3314-4 was engaged in shunting at the depot yard at Bad Muskau when it was photographed on 9th August 1973. Note the wooden shunting pole mounted alongside the boiler. (B.Rumary).

9.2.   Three years later, the unique Borsig 0-8-0T no. 99 3312-8 was similarly engaged on 8th September 1976. This locomotive was displayed on a plinth near Zittau until it was repatriated to its former home in 1995. (B.Rumary).

9.3. No. 99 3314-4 was viewed hauling a heavy coal train across the fields between Bad Muskau and Weisswasser on 9th August 1973. This was a typical example of the type of operation that existed throughout the existence of the line in its original form. (B.Rumary).

9.4. Another coal train was recorded departing from Bad Muskau, on this occasion hauled by Borsig 0-8-0T no. 99 3312-8. Due to the steep climb from the depot, a banking locomotive would often be employed, as on this occasion on 8th September 1976 although it was out of sight. (B.Rumary).

9.5. Orenstein & Koppel Feldbahn 0-8-0T no. 99 3311-6 was the banking locomotive of the coal train in the previous photograph. It was viewed carrying out its duty between Bad Muskau and Weisswasser. The coal in the last wagon appears to be comprised of more dust than solid fuel! (B.Rumary).

9.6. Two decades later and the Waldeisenbahn Muskau had been partially reopened as a tourist operation. The 1912 built Borsig 0-8-0T and a Jung 0-4-0T dating from 1938 were viewed at the depot south of Bad Muskau in October 1998, whilst being prepared for service. (J.Marsh).

9.7. On the same occasion, the Borsig 0-8-0T, formerly no.99 3312-8, was hauling a tourist train through the delightful surroundings of the country park, which has been created near Bad Muskau. The coaches have been constructed using the under frames of former freight wagons, many of which have remained as open topped vehicles. (J.Marsh).

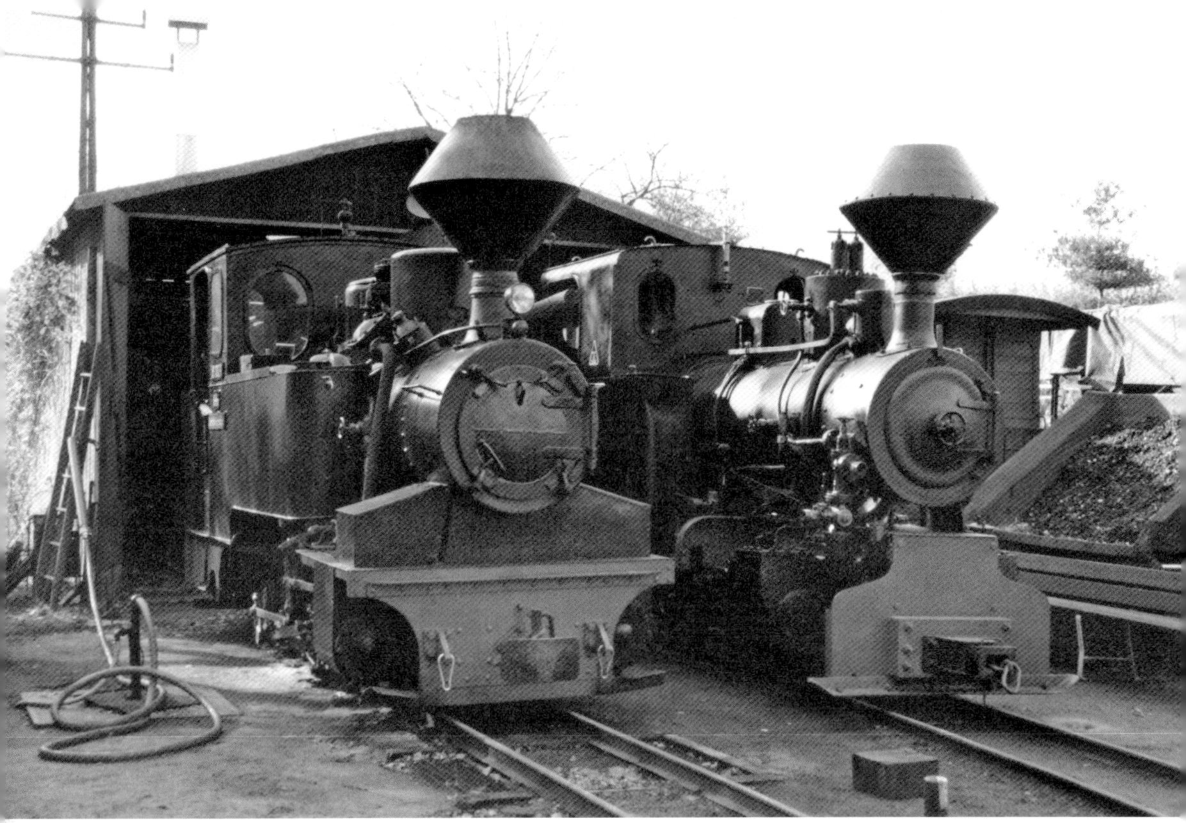

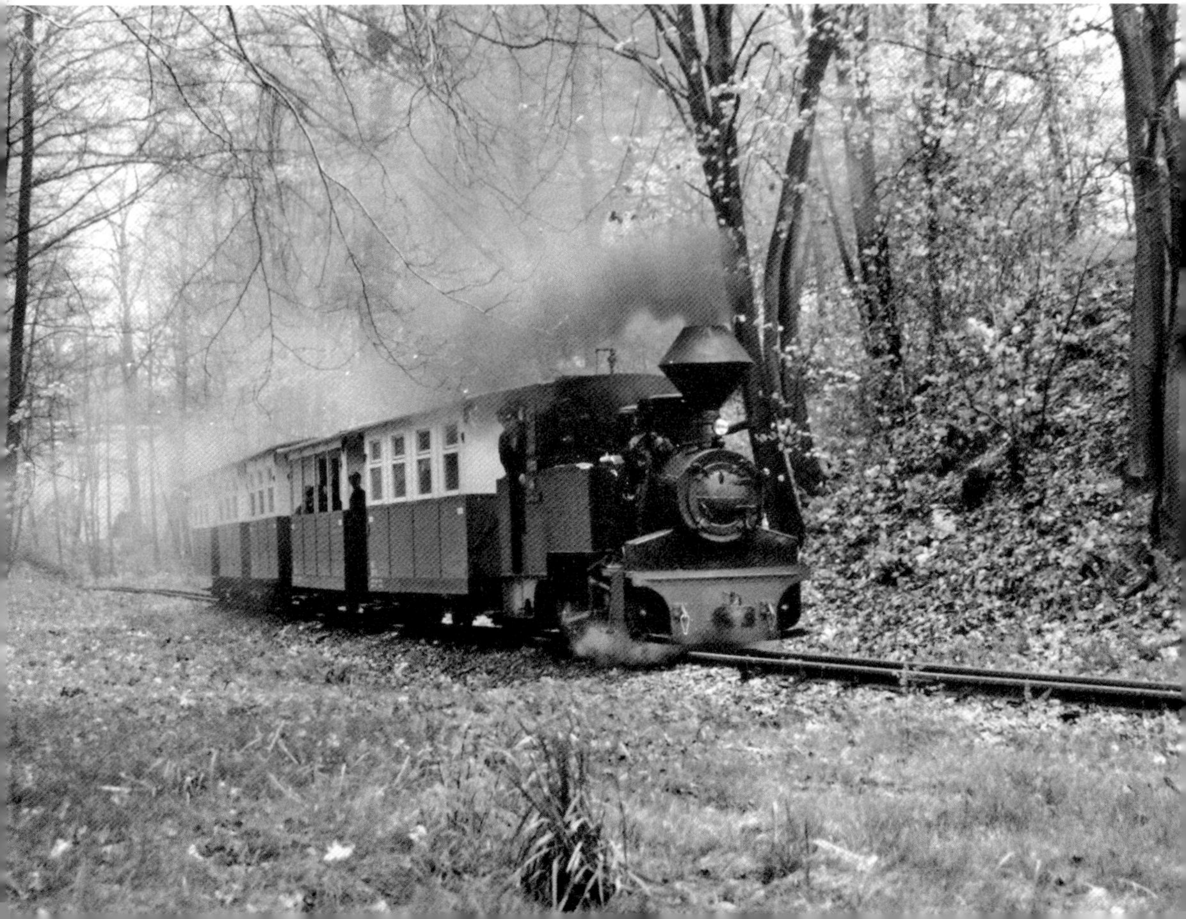

10. Sächsen Parkeisenbahnen

Germany has a long history of providing miniature railways in the parks of its major cities. The development of these fascinating lines, which were originally intended as short-term ventures in connection with major exhibitions, began in 1925. In that year Roland Martens, the Chief Engineer of the Krauss Light Locomotive Department at Munich, was asked to provide three locomotives and rolling stock for a 38cm (15 inch) line to be laid at the Munich Transport Exhibition. With no previous experience of building locomotives of such a small gauge, that were capable of hauling up to ten coaches with a total capacity of 160 passengers on gradients of 1 in 50, Martens consulted his old friend Henry Greenly for advice. The result was the famous K 3/6 Pacific design, which like Greenly's designs for the Ravenglass and Romney lines, were built to 1/3 scale although running on basically quarter scale track.

After the Munich exhibition closed, the three 4-6-2s were sold to Erich Brangsch, a locomotive dealer in Leipzig. Their new owner used the locomotives for further exhibitions throughout Europe including venues such as Rotterdam and Antwerp whilst two additional locomotives of the same type were supplied for an exhibition at Cork in 1932. In the meantime, six additional locomotives of the same design were supplied in 1928 for use on permanent miniature railways at Vienna and Seville. The three original K 3/6 locomotives, nos 001 – 003, returned to their homeland in 1930 and worked at new lines that had been recently constructed at Dresden and Leipzig. Two locomotives, nos 001 and 003, worked on the Dresden line until it closed in 1937 whilst no.002 was based at Leipzig until 1933 when it set off on its travels once again. During the 1930s, in conjunction with the Nazi propaganda programme, many large German cities staged exhibitions. Dresden and Leipzig were no exception and the Parkeisenbahnens were incorporated as an integral part of the exhibitions. The sight of the magnificent Martens K3/6 Pacific locomotives adorned with swastikas is something that the majority of people would prefer not to be reminded of, however it was part of the colourful career of these highly successful miniature locomotives.

In 1937 when three locomotives and additional rolling stock were required for an exhibition at Dusseldorf, the Krauss Light Locomotive Department had ceased to exist. With the newly formed Krauss-Maffei concern being unable to handle the order, three 4-6-2s of a similar design were supplied by Fried. Krupp. After the Dusseldorf line closed, the three Krupp locomotives were safely stored during the war and re-emerged in 1949 to work on a new line at Cologne. When this closed in 1953 the locomotives remained in store for two decades until they were acquired for use in the UK. Two now work at Bressingham whilst the third has joined the 4-6-2s that inspired the original design on the Romney, Hythe and Dymchurch. In 1950 Krauss-Maffei constructed two more locomotives to the original design for use at Stuttgart whilst a set of drawings were sent to India where the Tata Locomotive Works built another example for a line at Delhi.

Following World War Two when the cities of Germany were struggling to regain some resemblance of normality, the local governments of Dresden and Leipzig considered ways of providing suitable educational employment for schoolchildren during that difficult period. As a result the three original Brangsch locomotives were extracted from the quarry in which they had been safely stored since 1939 and restored to working order. The long disused lines at Dresden and Leipzig were rebuilt and both lines established in 1950 as Pioniereisenbahns, which were operated by schoolchildren between the ages of 9 and 16 under the guidance of Deutsche Reichsbahn. Locomotives nos 001 and 003 were returned to their former home at Dresden whilst no.002, following a short visit to a Garden Festival at Erfurt, returned to Leipzig.

In 1990 the two lines were renamed Dresdener Parkeisenbahn and LeipzigerParkeisenbahn Auensee respectively whilst still being operated by young people who perform virtually all the day to day running. The only exception is the actual driving and maintenance of the locomotives, although the youngsters are encouraged to assist their elders in the hope that in due course they may become qualified in those roles. The 5.6km Dresden line is considered to be the leading example of its type in Europe whilst the much shorter line at Leipzig with a length of 1.9km is somewhat overshadowed by its longer contemporary. However, both operate through areas of delightful parkland and are an object lesson in encouraging young people to learn skills and experience that otherwise would be denied to them.

Although the three original Martens locomotives are still working at Dresden and Leipzig, they have been assisted in recent years by more modern machines. The Dresden line has two battery electric locomotives, one of which is an articulated design supplied in 1982 based on a DR standard gauge diesel locomotive, whilst Leipzig has two diesel powered locomotives to assist the 4-6-2.

In addition to the 38cm Parkeisenbahn lines, three 60cm ventures of a similar nature were developed during the 1950s. A 2.3km line at Chemnitz was established in 1954 using former industrial motive power including a Riesa 0-4-0T and a powerful BoBo diesel. Two shorter lines at Görlitz and Cottbus used some of the equipment from the original Bad Muskau operation. The Cottbus line, which is located in the neighbouring state of Brandenburg, differs from the others in not being a circuit of the park in which it is situated. Instead it is an "out and back" operation which requires two locomotives, one of which is stabled at the top station in order to haul the train on the reverse leg. Motive power consists of Feldbahn 0-8-0Ts and the Krauss 0-6-0TT that was supplied to the Muskauer Waldbahnen in 1895.

10.1. The Reichgartenschäu at Dresden, now the Dresden Parkeisenbahn, recorded in the 1930s during a Nazi propaganda exhibition. Note the Krauss K 3/6 Pacific adorned with swastikas on the smoke box door. (K.Taylorson coll.)

10.2. Following the end of hostilities, the line was reopened as the Dresden Pioniereisenbahn in 1951 and operated mainly by schoolchildren. Krauss Pacific no.001 is seen about to depart from the principal station of the 5.6km line on 4th August 1963. (D.Trevor Rowe).

10.3. A young driver was busy shovelling fuel into the firebox of no.001, prior to leaving the station for another circuit of the line on the same occasion. (D.Trevor Rowe).

10.4. In 1990 the line was renamed Dresden Parkeisenbahn, although young people still play an active part in the operation. Krauss K 3/6 Pacific no.003 was recorded shortly before departing with a heavily patronised train on 23rd September 1995. (D.Trevor Rowe).

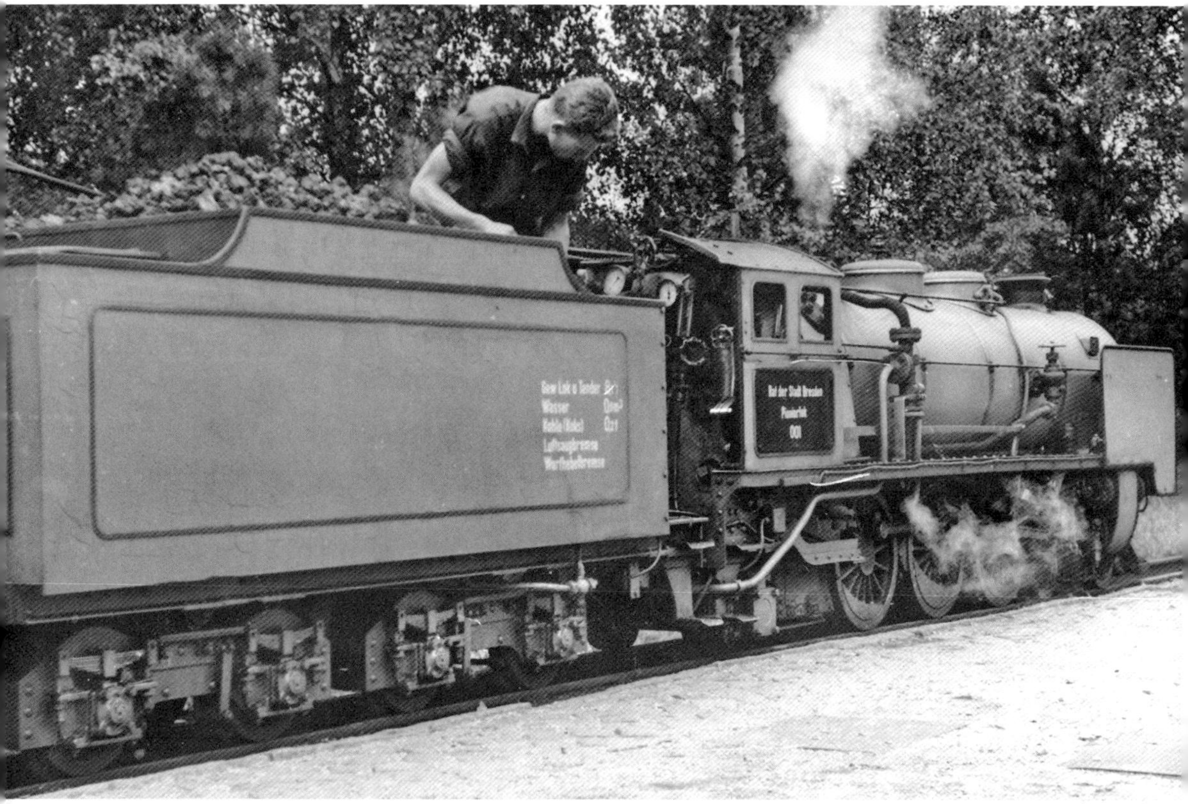

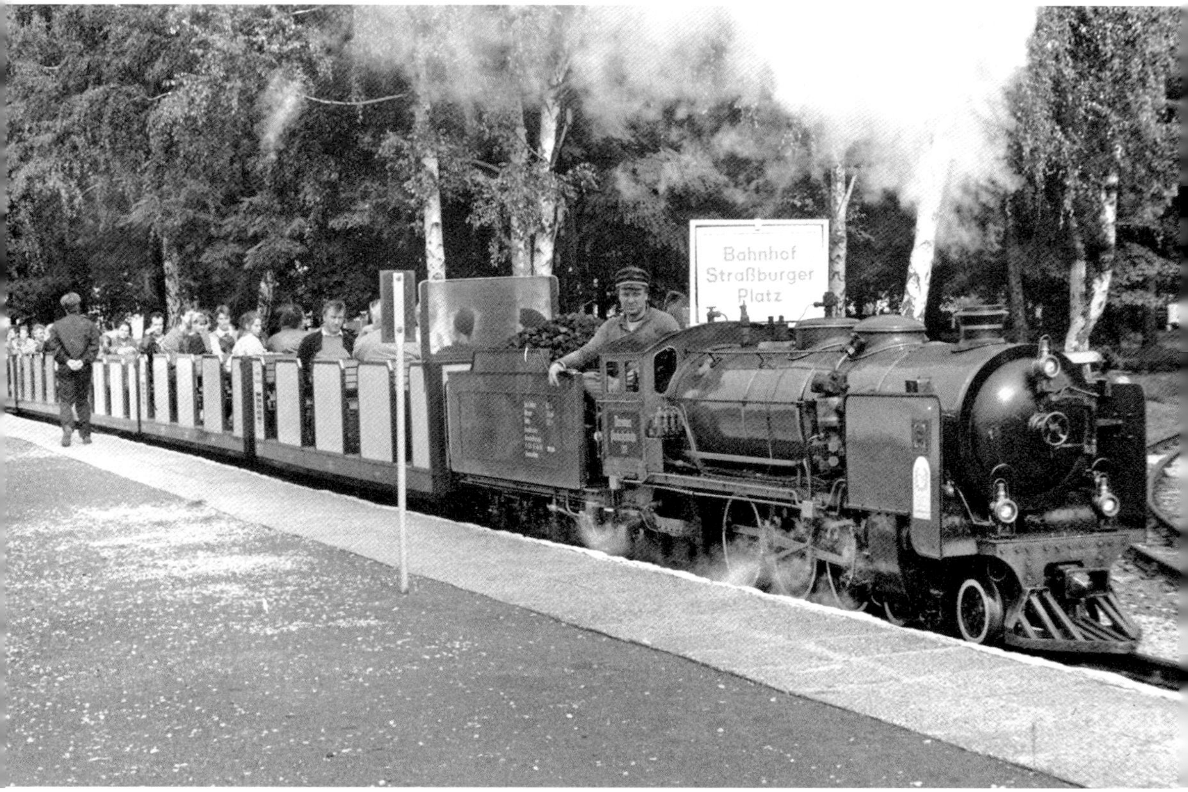
Bahnhof
Straßburger
Platz

10.5. The Parkeisenbahn Auensee at Leipzig has a similar history to the Dresden operation, although it has a much shorter route of 1.9km around a lake. One of the small diesel locomotives, that haul many of the trains, was viewed with the lake in the background on 10th September 2002. (D.Trevor Rowe).

10.6.   Krauss K 3/6 Pacific no.002 is depicted on the tickets issued by the Leipzig Parkeisenbahn Auensee. Some artistic licence has been employed as it shows the locomotive "floating" on the lake rather than making a circuit! (D.Trevor Rowe coll).

10.7.   The Cottbus operation opened in 1954 using redundant equipment from Bad Muskau, much of which was not required after the system was truncated in 1945. Krauss 0-6-0TT no.04 passes Feldbahn 0-8-0T no. 01 as it arrives at the top station whilst receiving a formal salute from a young station official on 8th September 1976. (B.Rumary).

10.8. On the same occasion, the Krauss 0-6-0TT drew to a halt at the platform of the top station whilst the Feldbahn 0-8-0T reversed onto the rear of the train, prior to hauling it back to the main station and depot situated at the lower end of the park. The line celebrated its 50th anniversary with a special gala event in June 2004. (B.Rumary).

POSTSCRIPT

Following the major political changes in Germany during the last decade, it is almost a miracle that any of the narrow gauge railways described in this publication have survived. Thanks to the intervention of dynamic private companies, the continued operation of the majority of lines that survived reunification has been achieved. Obviously the transport requirements of the 21st century are far removed from those even during the later years of the GDR, consequently the new operators are providing services more attuned to the tourist industry than daily transport needs. The fact that the systems have survived is a credit to the enthusiasm of their new owners.

Ffestiniog Travel, Harbour Station, Porthmadog, LL49 9NF (Tel:- 01766 516050) provide a comprehensive continental rail service. They can also assist in planning a "tailor made" itinerary to suit any individual requirements. Destinations in Germany are often included in their European holidays, including many of the lines covered in this publication. Tickets for the independent and museum railways listed below have to be purchased locally.

BVO Bahn, Fichtelbergbahn, Bahnhofstrasse 7, 09484 Kurort Oberwiesenthal, Germany. (Operators of the Cranzahl to Oberwiesenthal line.)

BVO Bahn, Lössnitzgrundbahn, Am Bahnhof 1, 01468 Mortizburg, Germany. (Operators of the Radebeul to Radeburg line.)

I.G.Pressnitztalbahn e.V, Am Bahnhof 78, 09477 Jöhstadt, Germany.

Museumbahn Schönheide / Carlsfeld e.V, Am Fuchsstein, 08304 Schönheide, Germany.

Pro Bahn – Regionalverband Oschatz e.V, Oschatzer Str.2a, 04769 Mügeln, Germany.

SOEG, Bahnhofstrasse 41, 02763 Zittau, Germany.

Sächsisches Schmalspurbahn-Museum Oberrittersgrün, Kirchstrasse 4 , 08355 Rittersgrün im Erzgebirge, Germany.

Middleton Press

Easebourne Lane, Midhurst
West Sussex. GU29 9AZ

A-0 906520 B-1 873793 C-1 901706 D-1 904474

OOP Out of Print at time of printing - Please check current availability **BROCHURE AVAILABLE SHOWING NEW TITLES**
Tel:01730 813169   www.middletonpress.com   email:info@middletonpress.co.uk

A
Abergavenny to Merthyr C 91 5
Aldgate & Stepney Tramways B 70 7
Allhallows - Branch Line to A 62 2
Alton - Branch Lines to A 11 8
Andover to Southampton A 82 7
Ascot - Branch Lines around A 64 9
Ashburton - Branch Line to B 95 2
Ashford - Steam to Eurostar B 67 7
Ashford to Dover A 48 7
Austrian Narrow Gauge D 04 7
Avonmouth - BL around D 42 X

B
Banbury to Birmingham D 27 6
Barking to Southend C 80 X
Barnet & Finchley Tramways B 93 6
Basingstoke to Salisbury A 89 4
Bath Green Park to Bristol C 36 2
Bath to Evercreech Junction A 60 6
Bath Tramways B 86 3
Battle over Portsmouth 1940 £16.95 A 29 0
Battle over Sussex 1940 A 79 7
Bedford to Wellingborough D 31 4
Betwixt Petersfield & Midhurst A 94 0
Blitz over Sussex 1941-42 B 35 9
Bodmin - Branch Lines around B 83 9
Bognor at War 1939-45 B 59 6
Bombers over Sussex 1943-45 B 51 0
Bournemouth & Poole Trys B 47 2 OOP
Bournemouth to Evercreech Jn A 46 0
Bournemouth to Weymouth A 57 6
Bournemouth Trolleybuses C 10 9
Bradford Trolleybuses D 19 5
Brecon to Neath D 43 8
Brecon to Newport D 16 0
Brickmaking in Sussex B 19 7
Brightons Tramways B 02 2
Brighton to Eastbourne A 16 9
Brighton to Worthing A 03 7
Bristols Tramways B 57 X
Bristol to Taunton D 03 9
Bromley South to Rochester B 23 5 OOP
Bude - Branch Line to B 29 4
Burnham to Evercreech Jn A 68 1
Burton & Ashby Tramways C 51 6

C
Camberwell & West Norwood Tys B 22 7
Canterbury - Branch Lines around B 58 8
Caterham & Tattenham Corner B 25 1
Changing Midhurst C 15 X
Chard and Yeovil - BLs around C 30 3
Charing Cross to Dartford A 75 4
Charing Cross to Orpington A 96 7
Cheddar - Branch Line to B 90 1
Cheltenham to Andover C 43 5
Chesterfield Tramways D 37 3
Chesterfield Trolleybuses D 51 9
Chichester to Portsmouth A 14 2 OOP
Clapham & Streatham Tramways B 97 9
Clapham Junction - 50 yrs C 06 0
Clapham Junction to Beckenham Jn B 36 7
Clevedon & Portishead - BLs to D 18 7
Collectors Trains, Trolleys & Trams D 29 2
Crawley to Littlehampton A 34 7
Cromer - Branch Lines around C 26 5
Croydons Tramways B 42 1
Croydons Trolleybuses B 73 1
Croydon to East Grinstead B 48 0
Crystal Palace (HL) & Catford Loop A 87 8

D
Darlington Trolleybuses D 33 0
Dartford to Sittingbourne B 34 0
Derby Tramways D 17 9
Derby Trolleybuses C 72 9
Derwent Valley - Branch Line to the D 06 3
Didcot to Banbury D 02 0
Didcot to Swindon C 84 2
Didcot to Winchester C 13 3
Douglas to Peel C 88 5
Douglas to Port Erin C 55 9
Douglas to Ramsey D 39 X
Dover's Tramways B 24 3
Dover to Ramsgate A 78 9

E
Ealing to Slough C 42 7
Eastbourne to Hastings A 27 4 OOP

East Cornwall Mineral Railways D 22 5
East Croydon to Three Bridges A 53 3
East Grinstead - Branch Lines to A 07 X
East Ham & West Ham Tramways B 52 9
East Kent Light Railway A 61 4
East London - Branch Lines of C 44 3
East London Line B 80 4
East Ridings Secret Resistance D 21 7
Edgware & Willesden Tramways C 18 4
Effingham Junction - BLs around A 74 6
Eltham & Woolwich Tramways B 74 X
Ely to Kings Lynn C 53 2
Ely to Norwich C 90 7
Embankment & Waterloo Tramways B 41 3
Enfield & Wood Green Trys C 03 6 OOP
Enfield Town & Palace Gates - BL to D 32 2
Epsom to Horsham A 30 4
Euston to Harrow & Wealdstone C 89 3
Exeter & Taunton Tramways B 32 4
Exeter to Barnstaple B 15 4
Exeter to Newton Abbot C 49 4
Exeter to Tavistock B 69 3
Exmouth - Branch Lines to B 00 6 OOP

F
Fairford - Branch Line to A 52 5
Falmouth, Helston & St. Ives - BL to C 74 5
Fareham to Salisbury A 67 3
Faversham to Dover B 05 7 OOP
Felixstowe & Aldeburgh - BL to D 20 9
Fenchurch Street to Barking C 20 6
Festiniog - 50 yrs of enterprise C 83 4
Festiniog in the Fifties B 68 5
Festiniog in the Sixties B 91 X
Finsbury Park to Alexandra Palace C 02 8
Frome to Bristol B 77 4
Fulwell - Trams, Trolleys & Buses D 11 X

G
Garraway Father & Son A 20 7 OOP
Gloucester to Bristol D 35 7
Gosport & Horndean Trys B 92 8 OOP
Gosport - Branch Lines around A 86 3
Great Yarmouth Tramways D 13 6
Greenwich & Dartford Tramways B 14 6
Guildford to Redhill A 63 0

H
Hammersmith & Hounslow Trys C 33 8
Hampshire Narrow Gauge D 36 5
Hampshire Waterways A 84 3 OOP
Hampstead & Highgate Tramways B 53 7
Harrow to Watford D 14 4
Hastings to Ashford A 37 1 OOP
Hastings Tramways B 18 9
Hastings Trolleybuses B 81 2 OOP
Hawkhurst - Branch Line to A 66 5
Hayling - Branch Line to A 12 6
Haywards Heath to Seaford A 28 2 OOP
Henley, Windsor & Marlow - BL to C 77 X
Hitchin to Peterborough D 07 1
Holborn & Finsbury Tramways B 79 0
Holborn Viaduct to Lewisham A 81 9
Horsham - Branch Lines to A 02 9
Huddersfield Trolleybuses C 92 3
Hull Trolleybuses D 24 1
Huntingdon - Branch Lines around A 93 2

I
Ilford & Barking Tramways B 61 8
Ilford to Shenfield C 97 4
Ilfracombe - Branch Line to B 21 9
Ilkeston & Glossop Tramways D 40 3
Industrial Rlys of the South East A 09 6
Ipswich to Saxmundham C 41 9
Isle of Wight Lines - 50 yrs C 12 5

K
Kent & East Sussex Waterways A 72 X
Kent Narrow Gauge C 45 1
Kingsbridge - Branch Line to C 98 2
Kingston & Hounslow Loops A 83 5
Kingston & Wimbledon Tramways B 56 1
Kingswear - Branch Line to C 17 6

L
Lambourn - Branch Line to C 70 2
Launceston & Princetown - BL to C 19 2
Lewisham & Catford Tramways B 26 X
Lewisham to Dartford A 92 4 OOP
Lines around Wimbledon B 75 8

Liverpool Street to Chingford D 01 2
Liverpool Street to Ilford C 34 6
Liverpool Tramways - Eastern C 04 4
Liverpool Tramways - Northern C 46 X
Liverpool Tramways - Southern C 23 0
London Bridge to Addiscombe B 20 0
London Bridge to East Croydon A 58 4
London Chatham & Dover Rly £7.95 A 88 6
London Termini - Past and Proposed D 00 4
London to Portsmouth Waterways B 43 X
Longmoor - Branch Lines to A 41 X
Looe - Branch Line to C 22 2
Lyme Regis - Branch Line to A 45 2
Lynton - Branch Line to B 04 9

M
Maidstone & Chatham Tramways B 40 5
Maidstone Trolleybuses C 00 1 OOP
March - Branch Lines around B 09 X
Margate & Ramsgate Tramways C 52 4
Marylebone to Rickmansworth D49 7
Midhurst - Branch Lines around A 49 5
Midhurst - Branch Lines to A 01 0 OOP
Military Defence of West Sussex A 23 1
Military Signals, South Coast C 54 0
Minehead - Branch Line to A 80 0
Mitcham Junction Lines B 01 4
Mitchell & company C 59 1
Moreton-in-Marsh to Worcester D 26 8
Moretonhampstead - Branch Line to C 27 3

N
Newbury to Westbury C 66 4
Newport - Branch Lines to A 26 6
Newquay - Branch Lines to C 71 0
Newton Abbot to Plymouth C 60 5
Northern France Narrow Gauge C 75 3
North East German Narrow Gauge D 44 6
North Kent Tramways B 44 8
North London Line B 94 4
North Woolwich - BLs around C 65 6
Norwich Tramways C 40 0

O
Orpington to Tonbridge B 03 0
Oxford to Moreton-in-Marsh D 15 2

P
Paddington to Ealing C 37 0
Paddington to Princes Risborough C 81 8
Padstow - Branch Line to B 54 5
Plymouth - BLs around B 98 7
Plymouth to St. Austell C 63 X
Porthmadog 1954-94 - BL around B 31 6
Porthmadog to Blaenau B 50 2 OOP
Portmadoc 1923-46 - BL around B 13 8
Portsmouths Tramways B 72 3 OOP
Portsmouth to Southampton A 31 2
Portsmouth Trolleybuses C 73 7
Princes Risborough - Branch Lines to D 05 5
Princes Risborough to Banbury C 85 0

R
Railways to Victory C 16 8
Reading to Basingstoke B 27 8
Reading to Didcot C 79 6
Reading to Guildford A 47 9
Reading Tramways B 87 1
Reading Trolleybuses C 05 2
Redhill to Ashford A 73 8
Return to Blaenau 1970-82 C 64 8
Roman Roads of Surrey C 61 3
Roman Roads of Sussex C 48 6
Romneyrail C 32 X
Ryde to Ventnor A 19 3

S
Salisbury to Westbury B 39 1
Salisbury to Yeovil B 06 5
Saxmundham to Yarmouth C 69 9
Saxony Narrow Gauge D 47 0
Seaton & Eastbourne T/Ws B 76 6 OOP
Seaton & Sidmouth - Branch Lines to A 95 9
Secret Sussex Resistance B 82 0
SECR Centenary album C 11 7
Selsey - Branch Line to A 04 5 OOP
Sheerness - Branch Lines around B 16 2
Shepherds Bush to Uxbridge T/Ws C 28 1
Shrewsbury - Branch Line to A 86 X
Sierra Leone Narrow Gauge D 28 4
Sittingbourne to Ramsgate A 90 8

Slough to Newbury C 56 7
Southamptons Tramways B 33 2 OOP
Southampton to Bournemouth A 42 8
Southend-on-Sea Tramways B 28 6
Southern France Narrow Gauge C 47 8
Southwark & Deptford Tramways B 38 3
Southwold - Branch Line to A 15 0
South Eastern & Chatham Railways C 08
South London Line B 46 4
South London Tramways 1903-33 D 10 1
St. Albans to Bedford D 08 X
St. Austell to Penzance C 67 2
St. Pancras to St. Albans C 78 8
Stamford Hill Tramways B 85 5
Steaming through Cornwall B 30 8
Steaming through Kent A 13 4
Steaming through the Isle of Wight A 56 8
Steaming through West Hants A 69 X
Stratford-upon-Avon to Cheltenham C 25
Strood to Paddock Wood B 12 X
Surrey Home Guard C 57 5
Surrey Narrow Gauge C 87 7
Surrey Waterways A 51 7 OOP
Sussex Home Guard C 24 9
Sussex Narrow Gauge C 68 0
Sussex Shipping Sail, Steam & Motor C 23
Swanley to Ashford B 45 6
Swindon to Bristol C 96 6
Swindon to Gloucester D46 2
Swindon to Newport D 30 6
Swiss Narrow Gauge C 94 X

T
Talyllyn - 50 years C 39 7 OOP
Taunton to Barnstaple C 60 X
Taunton to Exeter C 82 6
Tavistock to Plymouth B 88 X
Tenterden - Branch Line to A 21 5
Thanet's Tramways B 11 1 OOP
Three Bridges to Brighton A 35 5
Tilbury Loop C 86 9
Tiverton - Branch Lines around C 62 1
Tivetshall to Beccles D 41 1
Tonbridge to Hastings A 44 4
Torrington - Branch Lines to B 37 5
Tunbridge Wells - Branch Lines to A 32 0
Twickenham & Kingston Trys C 35 4
Two-Foot Gauge Survivors C 21 4 OOP

U
Upwell - Branch Line to B 64 2

V
Victoria & Lambeth Tramways B 49 9
Victoria to Bromley South A 98 3
Victoria to East Croydon A 40 1
Vivarais C 31 1

W
Walthamstow & Leyton Tramways B 65 0
Waltham Cross & Edmonton Trys C 07 9
Wandsworth & Battersea Tramways B 63
Wantage - Branch Line to D 25 X
Wareham to Swanage - 50 yrs D 09 8
War on the Line A 10 X
War on the Line VIDEO + 88 0
Waterloo to Windsor A 54 1
Waterloo to Woking A 38 X
Watford to Leighton Buzzard D 45 4
Wenford Bridge to Fowey C 09 5
Westbury to Bath B 55 3
Westbury to Taunton C 76 1
West Cornwall Mineral Railways D 48 9
West Croydon to Epsom B 08 1
West London - Branch Lines of C 50 8
West London Line B 84 7
West Sussex Waterways A 24 X
West Wiltshire - Branch Lines of D 12 8
Weymouth - Branch Lines around A 65 7
Willesden Junction to Richmond B 71 5
Wimbledon to Beckenham C 58 3
Wimbledon to Epsom B 62 6
Wimborne - Branch Lines around A 97 5
Wisbech - Branch Lines around C 01 X
Wisbech 1800-1901 C 93 1
Woking to Alton A 59 2
Woking to Portsmouth A 25 8
Woking to Southampton A 55 X
Woolwich & Dartford Trolleys B 66 9 OOP
Worcester to Hereford D 38 1
Worthing to Chichester A 06 1 OOP

Y
Yeovil - 50 yrs change C 38 9
Yeovil to Dorchester A 76 2
Yeovil to Exeter A 91 6

96